LEADING WELL

LEADING WELL

BECOMING A MINDFUL LEADER-COACH

Steve Gladis

Author of *Positive Leadership* and *Solving the Innovation Mystery*

ISBN-13: 9780989131421
ISBN-10: 0989131424
Library of Congress Control Number: 2017913178
Steve Gladis Leadership Partners, Annandale, VA

DISCLAIMER

I n simulated exchanges and examples, all names, characters, places, and incidents are the product of the author's imagination or are used fictionally. Any resemblance to actual persons (living or dead), businesses, organizations, events, or locales is entirely coincidental.

DEDICATION AND ACKNOWLEDGMENTS

This book is dedicated to George Mason University, without which I would never have written this or any other book. I've spent decades associated with this amazing university, as a student, a teacher, and a donor. Thanks to all my teachers, mentors, and colleagues, who taught me to "fly" well before I thought I could. Special thanks to Mason English professor Don Gallehr, director emeritus of the Northern Virginia Writing Project, who taught me to write, and went on to give me much more. Thanks to all the Mason presidents I have gotten to know: Angel Cabrera, Alan Merten, and George Johnson. Thanks to all the students I've been privileged to teach—especially for all they have taught me. Thanks to all the Mason schools, departments, and organizations I've been associated with: English, Education, Communication, the Center for the Advancement of Well-Being, and the Mason Enterprise Center. Thanks to all the donors, large and small, who continue to help Mason grow into a national and international powerhouse. And finally, thanks to the university's namesake, George Mason, for guiding us every day with his indomitable spirit of courage, vision, and service to our extraordinary nation.

L eadership is all about how you show up at work. And leaders who learn to be present in a mindful way rather than be distracted by regretful thoughts of the past or anxious thoughts of future develop great people, teams, and organizations. *Leading Well: Becoming a Mindful Leader-Coach* presents a road map for starting that journey to mindful leadership coaching. Here's an executive summary of the book.

How Does the Mind Work?

For the purposes of this book, the brain is defined as the physical organ, and the mind relates more to our abstract thoughts—it is the working brain. The brain operates on both emotional and rational levels. Often the emotional brain hijacks the rational brain and takes leaders and their teams on a mindless, unproductive, and even destructive ride. And one small structure, the amygdala, is at the center of it all. The amygdala sits in the middle of the emotional brain, the limbic system, and acts like a threat detector, much like a smoke alarm. It constantly scans for threats, both real and imagined. Unfortunately, the amygdala often reacts to mind-manufactured (imagined) threats where there are none, causing the brain to spiral into overreaction and dysfunction. Further, forceful leaders with authority and power who spiral out of control can seriously damage people, teams, and organizations. However, leaders who learn to become mindful can counteract this natural tendency to overreact to threats, especially the imagined ones. Jon Kabat-Zinn, the father of one of the most effective mindfulness programs in the world, Mindfulness-Based Stress Reduction (MBSR), defines it this way: "Mindfulness means paying attention in a particular way: on purpose, in the present moment, and nonjudgmentally."[1]

How Do You Become Mindful?

This chapter describes how you actually can become purposeful, present, and nonjudgmental—in other words, more mindful. Simply put: "Stress finds you. You have to go looking for relaxation," says David Gelles in *Mindful Work*. When leaders become stressed, they pass it along to their teams through emotional contagion that spreads like a psychological epidemic throughout the organization. How does that work? The body's sympathetic nervous system (SNS) is easily triggered by threats—both real and imagined—and this sets off a chemical cascade triggering the "fight-or-flight" reaction in the body. Conversely, the "rest-digest" parasympathetic nervous system (PNS)—triggered by mindful breathing—releases a whole array of calming and restorative rest-digest chemicals, the exact opposite of the threat response. The best way to switch the mind from fight-flight to rest-digest is to focus on rhythmic breathing. This is like the "big switch" that sets you on a new less reactive, more thoughtful track. The steps of mindful breathing are simply laid out in this chapter: first sitting quietly, breathing in and out; then, as the mind wanders, bringing it back to the breath, which exercises the mind's control over threats and brings it back to calm. The more you practice mindfulness, the greater your ability to control the fight-flight reaction. The more mindful you are, the more present you become as a leader.

How Is Mindful Leadership Coaching Used to Solve Problems?

Great leaders solve big problems. Some leaders engage in inefficient ways and dissipate energy if they follow some leadership models. However, efficient models build strength and energy. For example, there are autocratic, bureaucratic, charismatic, and democratic leadership models. Some leaders use a command-and-control approach, and others are "fixers," who strive to save people. Fortunately, there are options among the various models, and the coaching model has emerged as a powerful one that focuses on helping people solve their own problems. This leadership coach-approach not only saves a leader's energy but also builds employee engagement. The Leadership Problem-Solving Coaching Model helps develop leader-coaches, who assist others to solve their own problems. Based on the idea that the people closest to the problem possess the most current information and are the most likely to solve the problem, the coaching model follows four simple but powerful steps:

1. Problem: Get the person to accurately define the real problem or issue.
2. Present: Determine the current state and impact of the problem.

3. Possible: Examine the best possible future state, ideally what the future could look like.
4. Plan: Outline the first steps that move people toward the best possible state and become committed to the solution.

How Is Mindful Leadership Coaching Used to Develop Talent?

Talent development is at the heart of any successful business. No people, no mission. In a highly competitive world, companies must recruit, train, and retain talent. The ability to develop talent separates great leaders from the merely good. This is especially true today with baby boomers exiting the workplace in droves. Boomers are being replaced by millennials, who have both very different experience levels and a different view of work. Moreover, they are interested in frequent feedback, clear boundaries between work and play, and professional development. To adapt to this shift in worker philosophy, companies are adjusting their performance management systems.

Fortunately, with a simple adaptation, the leadership problem-solving coaching model provides an outstanding development and retention tool. First and foremost, the adaptation requires leaders to schedule periodic meetings with team members to discuss their careers. These should be conducted in an informal manner separate from performance appraisal sessions. Such meetings should happen two to four times a year. Further, a simple tweak of this leadership coaching model makes all the difference. Instead of starting with the problem, start with the possible. Here are the steps:

1. Possible (future): What do employees see as their best possible career state in the next year or two?

2. Present (state): Where are they now regarding readiness for the possible future state?
3. Problem: What must they do to get from the present to future state? Essentially, they need to answer the question: What is the gap between the present and possible future state?
4. Plan: What's the plan to move forward?

What's the first step, and how will their leader know they have done it? This developmental leadership coaching process might seem like a luxury or a burden for leaders; however, it provides the competitive edge in recruiting and retaining the talent of the future. Moreover, the more mindful and present the leader-coach and the coachee are during the coaching session, the better the solutions to problems.

How Is Mindful Leadership Coaching Used with Groups and Teams?

Several-to-One Coaching. While one-on-one coaching provides an opportunity to reflect and thoughtfully solve problems, several-to-one leadership coaching amplifies the experience. In essence, four to five people coaching one person happens best when one of the participants acts as the "managing coach," ensuring that the other coaches follow the coach-approach process by asking questions, not giving advice.

One-to-Many Coaching. If you've ever sat through an endless, painful, and rambling committee or staff meeting, one-to-many leadership coaching is for you. The two critical problems facing most group meetings, regardless of size, are a woeful lack of structure and the disruptive presence of dominant, overly aggressive personalities.

One-to-many coaching overcomes both of these issues. As in several-to-one coaching, one person must fill the role of "managing coach" to ensure that the group focuses on the four-step coach-approach process by asking questions rather than giving advice. This approach requires discipline and leadership, but the results are well worth the effort.

CONTENTS

INTRODUCTION

C ounter to common wisdom, I'll begin with a confession: I have spent much of my life in a mindless state. I'm a worrier, usually about future events that almost never materialize. As the French writer Montaigne once said, "There were many terrible things in my life and most of them never happened." One day, I decided to figure out the best way to deal with my anxiety, which ironically had helped me to accomplish a lot over the years but had also often drained my energy. I asked myself, How could I thrive in the present and neither fear some fictional future place, nor wallow in a memory-fogged past?

For many years, I listened to a meditation tape given to me by a wise woman, Dorie Hotis, who was well ahead of her time. However, I used that tape to fall into light twenty-minute naps. It was how I unwound every night before dinner. The light nap refreshed me, allowing me to be alert and present for the remainder of the evening. However, over the years, I fell out of this habit. For the past two years, I have been researching, learning, and practicing mindful meditation—striving to be fully awake and present wherever I am. Notice I said "practicing." I am still a work in progress.

To this end, I decided to take the Mindfulness-Based Stress Reduction (MBSR) program offered at Georgetown University. I chose to take MBSR instead of many other programs because it is taught at hundreds of medical schools and is based on scientific research.

The Georgetown program was led by Paul M. Jones, MD, a psychiatrist working at the university. I figured it would be a double bonus: meditation and perhaps some informal therapy on the side! Paul is fun-loving and gentle, but also firm, and an excellent teacher. Passionate about mindfulness, he is a great role model for its multiple benefits. While this book is not dedicated to him, it easily could have been. He deserves high praise and lasting thanks.

In this book, I shall try to summarize the relevant research and practice of mindfulness and why it is important to leaders. My hope is that this information will help leaders, especially the executives whom I coach almost every day, to discover the power of becoming a mindful leader-coach.

CHAPTER 1

How Does the Mind Work?

For eons, people have debated whether the mind and brain are the same thing. I won't take on the philosophers, but for the purposes of this book, the brain is defined as the physical organ, and the mind is where we hold our abstract thoughts. In a way, your mind is "your brain at work."[2] And yet it is more complex than that.

Let's start by understanding the process of neuroplasticity, the idea that you can change your brain throughout your life, regardless of age. You can change the structure of your brain. This can be done internally when interacting with and within ourselves, as well externally through interaction with others. For example, take a moment to think about anything. Maybe, think about your car. Now, think about it first with your right (relational) brain: Consider the contours, the feel of how it rides, and the smell of the leather. Next, consider the car from your left (linear/logical) brain: Flip through the owner's manual and read about the mileage in the city and on the highway, the navigation system's capabilities, the heating and air-conditioning system. As you honor these differences even within your own brain—right and left sections—and integrate them into a whole perception of your car, you begin to change your brain, ever so slightly but incrementally, with this new impression. Moreover, you can integrate the brain mindfully by giving it the time, space, and safety to honor differences and by allowing connection and integration to occur. Such integration allows new possibilities and creativity to emerge naturally.

On the other hand, think about times when you became rigid, when you did not honor differences or promote linkages and connections. For example, consider a bias you might have—let's say that, when talking in a group, you may tend to dismiss introverts in favor of more outgoing extroverts. I recall a group I coached years ago at a federal agency. The group was trying to untangle a complicated problem. One participant was a slight, quiet woman who was silent during the initial discussions of the group coaching/decision-making session. Finally, I asked her directly what she thought about the situation, and what she said was pure gold! From her thoughtful remarks, it was obvious that she had been listening intensely to everything discussed. And having listened to the discourse of others, she had formed a powerful opinion and expressed it. After her eloquent response, every time she spoke, it reminded me of an old EF Hutton commercial, where when this wise, older investment broker spoke, everyone stopped—frozen in anticipation of what was coming next.

What would have happened had I not asked for her opinion? Chances are good that the group would have pursued many unproductive trains of thought. As you reflect—by honoring differences and promoting linkages—well-being happens.[3]

To see how you might start the journey of reshaping your brain and integrating it, let's start with a simple exercise.

Try This Exercise

- Sit comfortably in your chair. With your feet on the floor and hands in your lap, soften your gaze or close your eyes, and just breathe in and out. Remain quiet for two minutes, doing nothing but breathing as rhythmically as possible.

- After you open your eyes consider the following:

    —How do you feel?

    —What thoughts floated in and out while you were sitting quietly? Were they thoughts of the past? Thoughts about the future?

    —How about thoughts about the present—thoughts about just sitting and breathing?

- Write down three words about how this simple exercise made you feel.

Sitting and breathing in silence is at the core of mindfulness because it calms down the amygdala and allows more of your brain to be present and available to solve problems. Congratulations! You have just taken the first step in the journey toward becoming a mindful leader-coach.

The Wandering Mind

Mark Williams, Oxford professor and founder of mindfulness-based cognitive therapy (MBCT), uses a powerful example straight from Animal Planet.[4] He focuses on the ubiquitous herds of gazelles roaming the Serengeti and how they run for their lives to avoid ravenous lions and then stop and resume grazing as if they had just paused to listen to a commercial on TV. This is not how humans react.

Recall 9/11 and how that horrible event heavily impacted all Americans for such an extended time. Remember how often you dwelled on the events of 9/11. Psychologists and psychiatrists told their patients to avoid rewatching those gruesome videos of the jets crashing into the Twin Towers to keep them from ruminating about the tragedy. This is not an easy thing to do, as we will discuss later.[5] And, simply asking the rational part of your brain to tell your emotional brain to "calm down" just annoys it! When we experience stress, as we did after 9/11, then a release, and then more stress, it produces a cascade of stress chemicals, such as adrenalin and cortisol into the bloodstream. It further creates a stress response that drags us into dissonance, an anxious state rooted in vigilance and self-protection.

The human brain is an evolutionary marvel. It took millions of years to form, so changing it isn't easy or fast. Moreover, the brain is particularly predisposed to remembering negative events—especially those that have significantly affected us, like physical injury and emotional trauma. In fact, we tend to "ruminate" or play back negative thoughts in our minds, and we can get caught in a non-stop negative loop. "The human mind is a wandering mind, and a wandering mind is not a happy mind," says Harvard psychologist Dan Gilbert.[6] Richard Boyatzis, who also researches the brain and teaches at Case Western Reserve, describes the wandering mind as a place where "dissonance is the default."[7]

Similarly, just as rumination about the past can cause the pain and suffering of regret and depression, fear of the future can trigger the agony of anxiety. Again, by focusing on the future, our brain prepares itself to cope with an uncertain future to protect us from potential harm. *What if I don't get my assignment in on time? What travel route should I take to get to an important meeting so I won't be late?* You get the idea. Overstressing about such future possible events, most of which rarely happen, leads to a constant and heightening sense of stress and anxiety.

While the fight-flight-freeze reaction may have originated millions of years ago at the sight of a predatory saber-toothed tiger, today's threats are far subtler, but no less threatening, to the mind. In fact, the mind often cannot distinguish between real and imagined threats. It's like when a false alarm goes off, firefighters don't know, and they must respond as if it were a blazing inferno.

Monkey Mind

We are incredibly preoccupied with work, family, career, and much more. In fact, we spend most of our time in a mindless state—often called "monkey mind," one that jumps around, either ruminating about the past or worrying about the future. Moreover, the world is full of endless distractions—the Internet, ever-present plasma screens, online games, and smartphones. And the net effect of such devices, especially smartphones, is that they keep us tethered to work. This overworks, overwhelms, overcommits, and exhausts us.[8] In fact, Americans are in contact with work seventy-two hours a week; 33 percent of us report extreme stress, pointed right at work; and, most of our visits to the doctor are stress-related complaints.[9] Monkey mind makes us mindless. And the best cure for mindlessness is to learn mindfulness.

What Is Mindfulness?

We frequently oscillate between stress and calm—often with an imbalance of time in a stressful state. However, just like our computers, there is a reset button available to everyone—mindfulness. Jon Kabat-Zinn, the founder of one of the most effective programs in the world, Mindfulness-Based Stress Reduction (MBSR), defines mindfulness this way: *"Mindfulness means paying attention in a particular way: on purpose, in the present moment, and nonjudgmentally."*[10] Let's break down this definition by examining the key phrases.

- **Paying Attention in a Particular Way:** How often have you had the TV turned on to watch a sports event while writing e-mails or texting at the same time? We call that multitasking, but psychologists call it task switching.[11] According to experimental psychologists, we can't multitask—do two things well at the same time. Rather, our mind merely switches from doing one task and then the other. However, while attempting to pay attention in this task-switching mode, we seriously degrade our functioning on both tasks.[12] That's why Kabat-Zinn was careful to define just how we need to pay attention, "in a particular way," which consists of being "on purpose, in the present moment, and nonjudgmentally."

- **On Purpose:** For centuries, Eastern philosophy has stressed the importance of being in the present by simply being silent and focused on the present moment. In the Western world, purposeful prayer has helped people focus on a similar kind of silent presence. And while mindful meditation has been associated with quasireligious overtones, *it is not religious.* Mindfulness simply requires focusing on your breathing and your body—on purpose. In fact, for over thirty years, people like Jon Kabat-Zinn have worked diligently to decouple mindfulness and meditation from religion. Mindfulness strives to purposefully keep your focus on the present moment—and nowhere else. That's harder than it appears, as you may have experienced from the two-minute opening exercise of just sitting and being in silence. And focusing on your breath provides an ever-present trigger to nudge you into mindfulness.

- **The Present Moment:** In reality, all we really have in life is the present moment or, as Eckhart Tolle refers to it, "The Now."[13] The present moment describes where we physically exist. And for many of us, the present moment—right here, right now—is usually good. Much of the time, where we are physically located is quite good—especially in developed countries. Our office or home is routinely warm enough in winter, cool enough in summer, and we have enough food and water. All that and more results in a good life. However, when our frenetic "monkey mind" kicks into gear, we start to think about the kids, the job, a looming deadline, and that good-life feeling fades fast. We forget about "being" in the moment and start thinking about the "doing" of life— the "should've, could've, would've" stuff. Invariably, we get pulled into either a future that will likely not happen or back to the past, which we cannot change. All of this happens at the expense of living in the present, where we exist right now.

- **Nonjudgmentally**: Humans are judgmental creatures. Every day, all day, we judge: whether we want this or that for lunch, if something is good or bad, right or wrong, or a threat or reward. Judgment is baked into our very DNA as a protective mechanism. However, all this judging, decision–making, and value creating is extremely tiring. After a day at work, most of us are ready to just "veg out," too tired to judge another thing. Moreover, life is full of ups and downs. What might feel like a big negative in the short term may turn out to be a very good thing in the long run. We all need time to develop perspective. Just think about that job you

REMEMBER THAT SOMETIMES NOT GETTING WHAT YOU WANT IS A WONDERFUL STROKE OF LUCK.
DALAI LAMA

didn't get, which led you to the great one you now have. Or, recall that time you took a detour and discovered something cool. Getting into a nonjudgmental, mindful state is like taking your brain to the gym, minus all the sweat! Mindfulness allows you to build a new muscle that opposes and balances against judgment. It is analogous to how the muscles of your stomach oppose your back muscles to maintain balance in your body. Otherwise, you fall out of balance and hurt your back! Even when we're quiet, our minds think about events, and we often put a "valence" (a positive or negative charge) on them, which results in a judgment. Meditation teaches us to notice thoughts, like clouds floating by the "sky" of our mind. Recognizing thoughts but not judging or dwelling on them is the essence of being mindful. And, no matter what floats by, recognizing it—even naming it—but then pulling your mind back to your breathing becomes the quest of mindfulness. While we never get perfect at it, the regular practice of mindfulness offers a lifetime of mental health and well-being much like consistent exercise offers lifelong physical health and well-being.

Try This Exercise

Let's try another simple meditation exercise. Sit comfortably in your chair. Feet on the floor, hands in your lap, soften your gaze or close your eyes, and just breathe, in and out. This time, when you notice thoughts floating by like clouds in the sky, acknowledge them but let them float by and return your attention to your breath. And just remain quiet for about three minutes. Try it now.

OK.

How did that feel?

Did your thoughts float by while you were sitting quietly?

Were your thoughts about the past or the future?

How about thoughts regarding the present—just sitting and breathing?

Chances are that you had thoughts about all the above, and that's what the mind does—it wanders. And such mindful exercise recognizes and honors the mind's wandering. At the same time, mindfulness brings back the mind to the present by concentrating on our breathing, which returns us to the body and the present moment. And that exercise of bringing the mind back to the breath is like doing a repetition with a weight—you build the mindfulness "muscle."

Sitting, focused on your breathing in silence, is at the very heart of mindfulness.

What's the Impact of Mindfulness?

David Gelles, a writer for the *New York Times*, is a lifelong meditator and student of mindfulness. In his recent book, *Mindful Work: How Meditation Is Changing Business from the Inside Out*, Gelles makes particularly strong arguments for the impact of the practice of mindfulness on ourselves, our daily lives, and, especially, on our work:

- **Impact on the Brain:** Mindfulness meditation thickens the prefrontal cortex (executive center) of the brain, which is responsible for positive behavior and appropriate responses. This practice also stimulates the hypothalamus, which increases learning and memory in the brain, and produces a substance called GABA (gamma-aminobutyric acid) that shrinks and dulls the effects of the amygdala (the brain's fire alarm), making us less likely to overreact to stress. Kids in school who practice mindfulness pay better attention and possess better control over their emotions. Prosocial behavior is a direct result of meditation in both kids and adults. In short, we become better human beings when we meditate.

- **Impact on Health**: "Stress finds you. You have to go looking for relaxation," Gelles tells us. Stress helped us survive and evolve as humans. Today, however, instead of protecting us from a saber-toothed tiger, an overactive amygdala results in heart disease, cancer, diabetes, depression and anxiety, fatigue, and muscle pain. Highly stressed people are more excitable, less productive, and have prohibitively expensive health-care costs. Mindfulness reduces cortisol levels, aids the immune system, increases happiness, and calms you down. In short, mindfulness increases your resilience! Just as stress is contagious, so too is mindfulness—especially if you're a leader.

- **Personal**: Meditation calms the anxious and depressed brain, reduces stress levels, and makes us more compassionate toward others. Mindfulness even overcomes the "bystander effect" by threefold! Instead of ignoring people in trouble, mindful people step in and step up. Stress is not triggered by what is happening in our lives but by how we respond to it. "Between stimulus and response there is a space. In that space is our power to choose our response. In our response lies our growth and our freedom," notes Viktor Frankl, famed psychiatrist and Holocaust survivor.[14]

- **Corporate Impact**: Mindfulness adds to the quadruple bottom line: profits, society, environment, and employees' emotional well-being. Google, General Mills, Aetna, LinkedIn, Twitter, Goldman Sachs, Genentech, Ford, Cisco, and many other leading companies have adopted meditation-based programs to calm executive minds, which contribute to better leadership. In short, mindfulness is good for business, and many top companies have figured that out.

- **Sports**: Very successful coaches use mindfulness for a competitive advantage. Phil Jackson used meditation to help both the Chicago Bulls and the LA Lakers win eleven NBA Championships between them! He taught mindfulness to Michael Jordan, Scottie Pippen, Kobe Bryant, and Shaquille O'Neal. In teaching players to be mindful moment by moment, Jackson taught his players how to let go of bad shots or botched plays, which helped them bounce back from disappointments. Pete Carroll of the Seattle Seahawks also uses mindfulness techniques with his team.

- **Learning**: We are hardwired to have a wandering mind—it's evolutionary and protective. However, as mentioned previously, "A human mind is a wandering mind, and a wandering mind is an unhappy mind" (Gilbert). Experiments with mindful high-school and college kids showed improved memory and test results. The practice of mindfulness raised average SAT scores by seventy points; lowered anxiety, depression, anger, and fatigue; and produced better immune reactivity.[15]

Why Is Mindfulness Important to Leaders?

Obviously, everyone assigns differing degrees of value to all sorts of issues, like stress, happiness, and mindfulness. What makes such differing value assignments critical for leaders and their followers? Some research on the nature of authority, coupled with findings in neuroscience, may help us understand better.

Authority

Authority has a powerful influence on followers: Leaders *are* the difference. They make the most difference because of their authority—for good or bad.[16] One classic study, the Milgram experiment—named after the psychologist leading the study—highlighted the power of leaders over followers in the form of a social science experiment at Yale in the 1960s. The experiment centered on obedience to authority figures. People designated as "learners" (wired with electrodes) sat in a booth removed from the "teachers," who were male volunteers from the local New Haven community. A lead "experimenter" in a white lab coat oversaw the experiment. Whenever a learner got a question wrong, the learner was shocked by the teacher. As part of the experiment, the shocks got incrementally more severe and evoked intense emotional pleas from learners to cease the pain and suffering. Teachers (remember they were locals from New Haven) became overwrought because their punishing actions were in direct contrast with their social mores and values. However, at the insistence of the experimenter (the doctor in charge), these teachers administered the shocks up to levels that could have killed the learners!

Now, here's the rest of the story: The experimenter (the head authority figure) was not a real doctor; rather, he was an actor in the study hired to portray the role of chief experimenter. Moreover, the "learners" were also actors, and the electrodes were not connected to any electrical currents—the actors merely pretended to be shocked. However, the "teachers" were indeed local people (the real subjects of the study). Indeed, prime purpose of this study was to isolate the effect of authority—to see how far healthy, well-adjusted, upper-middle-class citizens responded to authority. And the results were that a large percentage (65 percent) of the participants acted just like the Nazis in Germany who did terrible, unspeakable things to Jews in concentration camps but claimed (at the Nuremburg war trials) that the only reason they did it was because they were just following orders from a higher authority. This is a tragic, but amazing, example of authority's power over us and has been labeled as the "Nuremburg defense." Eventually, this was nullified as a legitimate defense.

In a study referenced in the book *Influence,*[17] a similar phenomenon called "Captainitis" emerged. During a flight-simulator retraining experiment, captains were told by experimenters to perform a catastrophic maneuver not long after the crew began the simulated flight. The captain was to do something not only catastrophic but also something that the crew would know was dangerous and potentially deadly. Amazingly, despite the fact that crews knew what was going on, a whopping 25 percent of the crews did not challenge the captain. That's one in four of every flight crew! A rather sobering thought for the next time you fly.

There are numerous other examples in daily life about authority's influence. Just look at the power and influence that CEOs, doctors, teachers, ministers, priests, coaches, and many others have over people who are or feel subordinate to them. Newspapers are full of examples of how that power can be misused, ranging from corruption to coercion to sexual exploitation and abuse.

Next, let's explore what happens in the brain that makes it critical for leaders to be present in the moment, in a particular way, and nonjudgmentally. In short, when it comes to leaders, emotions beget emotions, both positive and negative.

Neuroscience: The Brain—An Open System

Employing the MRI and fMRI, neuroscience has revealed extraordinary secrets of the brain. To protect us, our brains are hardwired to warn us of potential threats in the environment. As mentioned previously, in the middle of our brains sits an almond-shaped primal mechanism called the amygdala. Two amygdalae, one each in the right and left hemispheres, work together as a unit.

The amygdala is always on and picking up signals, especially from the leader. As part of the limbic system—our primitive, ancient brain—the amygdala stimulates the injection of chemicals and hormones for fight or flight into the body, activating the sympathetic nervous system. The basic primal question that the amygdala asks is, will this threat eat me, or can I eat it?[18] If we perceive something as a threat, we will focus on it intently, which narrows our scope, creativity, and ability to think of innovative solutions.[19] Our eyesight provides an excellent analogy. Our normal, relaxed peripheral vision offers about 180 degrees of lateral panoramic vision. When relaxed, we need to only modestly rotate our heads to see all around us. In karate, this is called "soft eyes" and allows confident and calm black belts to "see" attacks coming at them from anywhere in the room.

Unfortunately, according to Richard Boyatzis and Annie McKee in *Resonant Leadership,* when we get overstressed through the grind of threat after threat in our fast-paced world, we tend to invest more and more of ourselves—called the sacrifice syndrome—to keep things afloat. Eventually, all the stress pushes us into a state of negativity called "dissonance." Resulting from continued stress, dissonance produces poor judgment, disharmony, and ultimately dysfunction. In dissonance and under threat, our attentional focus can narrow to as little as thirty degrees (cognitive tunneling), depending on the severity of the threat. Under threat, we get fixated only on what's right in front of us and often make poor decisions because we lack the advantage of attentional peripheral vision: greater data input.

You may recall the movie *Jurassic Park* and how the dangerous raptors stalked their prey. One raptor would show up in front of the prey, essentially freezing it in its tracks. The prey's focus narrows down thirty degrees, riveted on the rapture preparing to attack. Then, suddenly, a second raptor attacks from the side and kills the prey—precisely because the prey was cognitively fixated on the raptor right in front of it.

When we are in dissonance, we become fixated on the threat. However, today that threat is no longer simply a physical threat but is instead a mental one, such as a boss's complaint, an overdue report, a missed sales quota, and the like. And in the state of dissonance caused by constant stress, we are out of tune! Here's one surefire test of whether you're in the state of dissonance: you think that everyone around you is a "jerk" and not pulling their weight—except, you, of course!

Unfortunately, dissonance is not a rare condition. Rather for all of us, according to Boyatzis, dissonance is the default.[20] Why? Because the amygdala is always on alert! It's hardwired into our brains to detect threats of all sorts, real and imagined. Remember the Montaigne quote offered earlier: "There were many terrible things in my life and most of them never happened." As a leader, you must work to counter this dissonance default due to its effects on you, your colleagues, and your followers. Stress creates tunnel vision and makes leaders vulnerable to huge judgment errors and costly mistakes. Dissonant leaders jump to conclusions, get defensive, and trigger stress in themselves and others. Comedian Danny Thomas once said that he knew a woman whose favorite position was "beside herself" and whose preferred sport was "jumping to conclusions." She was clearly in a state of dissonance! In addition, because of the power of authority, leaders are like the Wi-Fi "hot spots" found at places such as Peet's, Panera, or Starbucks! These leadership hot spots broadcast a strong signal that gets picked up by the wireless network connectors in the brains of followers. When leaders are far away, like with our cell phone's Wi-Fi connectors, we only feel one or two "bars" of reception. Their influence is not strong. But when leaders are close, raise their voices, or display emotion, our brains magnify their output and pick up all five bars of connectivity from their authority Wi-Fi hot spot. It's been said that, in the minds of followers, leaders do not have voices but microphones, and they do not have suggestions but demands. Leaders set the mood and tone of the workplace and, over time, can change the climate or personality of the organization. Thus, working around a depressed leader can depress you. Working around a positive leader can make you more positive.[21]

Indeed, emotions—positive and negative—spread quickly. Think about the last time your son or daughter was deeply hurt by someone and brought that emotional baggage home to you, and then you told your spouse or friend, and so on. Depending on the severity of the incident, any number of people are affected by the original transgression, the influence of which grows quickly and exponentially over time. In fact, leaders create an emotional wake, called an "emotional contagion," that can spread either as a positive force or negative virus.[22] And, good or bad, leaders have a strong effect on followers' moods, emotions, and mind-sets. Negativity leads to disengagement and, potentially, a 30 percent lack of productivity.[23]

On the other hand, mindful, positive leaders spread a mood of trust and openness, which can lead to creativity and cognitive ease. This creates the ability to think without restraints and the potential to generate several options to solve important problems by reflection, rather than by overreacting.[24] Barbara Frederickson, a psychologist and professor at the University of North Carolina, espouses a theory called "broaden and build."[25] She notes that stress creates tunnel vision (cognitive tunneling) and makes us vulnerable to judgment errors and mistakes—being blindsided. We jump to conclusions, get defensive, and create stress in ourselves and others. However, under her broaden-and-build schema, positivity creates a safe place and opens the mind allowing us to listen, learn, and solve problems better and faster.

Unfortunately, most of us live in a mindless state, not in a mindful, broaden-and-build state. And when you're a mindless leader, you create a stress wave, sometimes a stress tsunami, that can crash through an organization, causing irreparable damage. Consider, for example, when the Supreme Court issued their order against Bell Telephone.[26] A surge of uncertainty and stress crashed through that organization, resulting in many people getting laid off, getting ill, and an overreaction to the incredible stress.

Rethinking Stress

Stress is real and always present at some level or other. Ironically, a total lack of stress is death! Fortunately, Stanford Professor Kelly McGonigal has studied how to use stress to our advantage. In her book, *The Upside of Stress: Why Stress Is Good for You and How to Get Good at It*,[27] McGonigal emphasizes that stress can be both bad and good for you, depending on how you think about stress—it's all about your mind-set. Stress can make you sick if you let it overwhelm you, or you can reach out and help someone else and find yourself refreshed. You can become depressed, isolated, and selfish, or you can exercise compassion and altruism, and, suddenly, you are tending and befriending instead of fighting or fleeing. Talented athletes, successful students, and high-performing professionals who have had their mind-sets "reset" with incredibly simple interventions can reach higher levels of performance while under stress. The latest science on stress shows that it can make us smarter, stronger, happier, as well as more courageous and compassionate—not quite what you may have thought. Indeed, the advice from science is as simple as it is counterintuitive: Don't avoid stress, but "rethink and embrace it." And if you do, you will get what you expect.

CHAPTER 2

How Do You Become Mindful Leader?

As kids, you may have played the game called follow the leader, in which the leader at the head of a line of followers moves about and then does something physical, like raises both arms and waves, and you must mimic it or become eliminated from the game. In truth, leaders have always been the ones we mimic. It's a survival adaptation—we mimic the leader to remain in the tribe. Unfortunately, some leaders exhibit poor behavior—like being overreactive and unthoughtful, and that negative behavior gets replicated as well. Mindful leaders produce mindful followers and eventually a mindful organization predisposed to thoughtful decisions. But that takes both a willingness and practice.

If you have ever tried to get in shape, you may have included push-ups as part of your fitness regimen. In the beginning, you may only be able to do three push-ups correctly. However, with perseverance, you will be able to build capacity and do many more push-ups in a few short weeks. You're building capacity in the relevant muscles to do push-ups correctly.

That same capacity-building process takes place in the mind. We build mindful capacity when we learn how to work out the brain and become more mindful. The mindfulness builder that takes you to a "stronger brain" is mindful breathing or meditation in the moment, in a particular way, and nonjudgmentally—to again reference Jon Kabat-Zinn.

Now, let's do it!

Try This Being-Quiet Exercise

We are going to repeat the exercise that we did at the beginning of this book. Find a quiet place where you will not be disturbed for the next five to ten minutes. Find a good straight-back chair—a kitchen or dining-room chair will work just fine. Set the timer on your cell phone for five minutes; use a gentle chime alarm or soft, classical music. Remember we are trying to build the mind muscle. Let's get started.

1. Sit comfortably in your chair. Have your feet on the floor and your hands in your lap; close your eyes, and just breathe in and out. Now, remain quiet.
    (a) Thoughts will float in and out of your mind as you breathe. Simply treat them like clouds floating by—your mind is the sky. Some clouds will be bigger than others. Just acknowledge them, and then go back to concentrating on your breathing, in and out.
    (b) The breathing will transport you from your thinking mind (often overactive) to your feeling mind—your body-based mind.
2. When your timer chimes, take a couple of deep breaths and open your eyes slowly.
3. How did that feel? Where did your mind go to? Did your thoughts float in and out while you were sitting quietly? Were your thoughts about things that happened in the past, present, or the future?
4. (*Sitting and breathing in silence is the key to mindfulness.*)

Recall that we discussed the idea of using your breath as a switching mechanism, a trigger, so to speak. Your breath is always working and available to you; if not, you have a much bigger problem than trying to master mindfulness! In essence, the ever-present physical act of breathing makes it a perfect trigger for the practice of mindfulness. On the other hand, the problem is that breathing is also automatic. As mentioned earlier, the autonomic nervous system ensures that our body keeps working, like an automatic pilot. You don't have to concentrate to keep your blood flowing or your breath working—it is automatic.

However, when you concentrate on your breath, good things can happen. First, this infuses the body with oxygen, the body's lifeline. No oxygen, no mindfulness, no nothing! Second, when you concentrate on the rhythm of your breathing, exhaling in and out, the autonomic nervous system switches from the sympathetic nervous system—the vigilant sentinel that warns us of threats and pushes us to fight or flight—to the parasympathetic system, which causes us to rest, digest, and relax. Essentially, when you begin to focus on your breathing, you switch mental tracts from the "monkey brain," darting around trying to find threats, to your body, rooted in the here and now, that allows you to sit with no agenda, no judgment, and no pressing need to be anywhere else.

The Physiology of the Stress and Rest Responses

As Richard Boyatzis explains in *Resonant Leadership*, when we were hunters on the plains thousands of years ago, we rallied the tribe to hunt for food. And trying to take down a wooly mammoth would spike the adrenalin in anyone's system! During the hunt, heart rates elevated and adrenalin pumped into our hearts to ready us for a fight; further, the hormone cortisol got pumped into our muscles to protect us from pain and bleeding—the fight-flight syndrome emerged in full force.

However, once the hunt was over, the time came for eating, resting, and digesting. Think of that period as resembling our modern-day weekend, when we rest and prepare for the new week. This period is important to restore our bodies and minds to health. We toggle between fight-flight to rest-digest.

The following explanation comes from my latest book, *Smile. Breathe. Listen: The 3 Mindful Acts for Leaders*[28]:

> Basic bodily functions like breathing, circulation, neural response, digestion, and others all work without us actively thinking about them or cognitively controlling them. In short, they're all on autopilot, also known as the autonomic nervous system.

As mentioned previously, the autonomic nervous system is divided into two branches: the sympathetic and parasympathetic nervous systems. Let's explore those two systems in more depth.

The sympathetic nervous system (SNS) controls the body's fight-flight primal response to any threat. Let's say someone throws a baseball at you when you are not ready, but you catch sight of it at the last moment and duck as you hear it whiz by your ear. That's the SNS at work. If you stopped to think, "Hmm, there's a ball coming my way!" you would get beaned!

In more sophisticated situations, when there is time, the SNS engages the prefrontal cortex (PFC), which acts like a firewall between the fast-acting amygdala (the brain's fire alarm) and any actions you might take. Chronic stress leads to the thinning of the PFC, the executive function of the brain that helps us make good decisions. Such thinning of the PFC makes you more vulnerable to stress and more likely to be a "carrier" of stress to others, especially if you are a leader. At the same time, chronic stress exacerbates the amygdala, which triggers more stress, elevating blood pressure, increasing stress hormones, and hurting the immune system. Such effects have a negative effect not only on us but also on anyone in our proximity.

The PFC (located right behind your forehead) also acts as a kind of "flight simulator," as Harvard's Dan Gilbert[29] calls it, because it can conjure up all sorts of images as our brains try to interpret and practice potential acts. It's an evolutionary device to keep us safe. If we watch one person attempt to jump across a puddle and not make it without getting wet, we do a simulation in our own mind to decide whether we will jump or not.

The second part of the autonomic system, the parasympathetic system (PNS), focuses on the body and switches off the SNS emotional surge, allowing us to consider options under pressure. If the SNS is the fight-or-flight trigger in our brain, then the PNS is the rest-and-recover section of our brain. Psychologist Rich Hanson[30] puts it this way: "Triggering the PNS, often through long slow breathing, switches the mind from fight-or-flight to rest-and-digest as it slows down heart rate, increases intestinal activity, and relaxes muscles in the gastrointestinal tract."

The Big Switch: Mindful Breathing

Fortunately, we can all take advantage of what I call "the big switch": mindful breathing. Simply focusing on your breath calms your mind and body. For thousands of years, Eastern monks have studied the process of focusing on breathing; they call it "meditation." Modern neuroscience and brain scan studies demonstrate that being in the present moment and focusing on your breath calm your mind and allows you to make better decisions. Brain scans and interviews with trained psychologists indicate that meditators, or mindful breathers, are among the happiest people in the world.[31]

There's a lesson here for us all. Yet because meditation has been associated with Buddhism, many Westerners treat meditation as an Eastern religious practice or worse, just hocus-pocus. Wrong! I would like to adopt a new way of discussing the topic: mindful breathing.

Try This Exercise: Switching Tracks

In this exercise, all we will do is practice switching from flight-flight to rest-digest using breath as the trigger to change states:

- Think of something, either positive or negative, going on in your life right now. Maybe it's an accomplishment, a failure, a happy moment, or a sad one.
- Now, hold your breath for twenty-five seconds on a count of three. Check your timer on your phone…one, two, three—go.
- Exhale—how did that feel? During that time, especially in the last ten seconds, were you still thinking about the positive or negative thing going on in your life? Probably not! This simple-but-powerful exercise points out two things. First, it keeps things in perspective—*breathing trumps everything*. No breathing means no meditation, no worrying, no celebration, no living! Second, it shows how quickly you can shift your mind and switch your mental tracks, so to speak.
- I'm not necessarily advocating holding your breath to start meditation. However, I will strongly suggest it if you have trouble cleansing your mind from a lot of intrusive thoughts.

Developing a Practice of Mindfulness

The word "practice" has at least two primary definitions:

1. "The actual application or use of an idea, belief, or method as opposed to theories about such application or use."[32] Example: *It's important to understand the principles and practices of teaching.*
2. "The repeated exercise in or performance of an activity or skill to acquire or maintain proficiency in it." Example: *You must practice to get better at tennis.*

To understand mindfulness, both definitions are useful. First, mindfulness is taking an idea or a theory and applying it in the real world—where the rubber meets the road. If we can't use mindfulness to help in our daily lives, it becomes an interesting, but hollow, concept. Second, it takes repetition and practice to acquire any skill, whether it's tennis or mindfulness.

As mentioned before, mindfulness is like taking your brain to the gym for a workout—much like lifting weights or running. In fact, some believe that mindfulness will become the next health craze, like running was in the 1980s and '90s. All sports and habits require three things: training, practice, and application.

Training

When you want to develop your body in a sustainable, balanced way, you need to develop muscular strength, flexibility, and cardio fitness. When you have all three, the chances of injury, fatigue, or loss of interest diminish. However, if you either lack or overdevelop just one of these, you will have an imbalance that causes problems. So too, with mindfulness—proper training is required.

Moreover, at the heart of training is knowledge, which can come from many sources, including coaches.

Coaches

To start, you must know how to become mindful. It is a natural skill we had before today's electronic distractions invaded our lives. To reexperience that place, just go to a remote retreat with no Internet or TV. It might drive you nuts at first, but wait and see what happens. We must learn (or relearn) this fundamental skill of unplugging.

The fast track to learning anything, even mindfulness, is a good coach—someone who knows the skill and is willing and able to teach it to you. Mindfulness coaches teach people to become more conscious about their breathing by incorporating the training into the four formal practices of MBSR training program mentioned earlier—the body scan, sitting meditation, mindful movement, and mindful eating. During the body scan, participants breathe consciously, slowly, and deeply while focusing their attention on scanning their body from heel to head. This self-awareness promotes locating, identifying, and releasing tension. During sitting meditation, participants focus on slow, deep breathing, while they concentrate on relaxation. Mindful movement involves gentle stretching exercises performed slowly with the rhythm of the breath paired with body movement. In mindful eating, participants breathe slowly using all their senses, that is, sight, touch, smell, hearing, and taste, to experience their food. This process allows them to enjoy eating, rather than rushing to finish. Studies conducted to assess the effects of MBSR on health outcomes report that use of MBSR reduces pain, anxiety, and depression in various patient populations, for example, patients with fibromyalgia, irritable bowel syndrome, and cancer.[33]

Doing and Being

Leaders have two jobs: doing and being. Unfortunately, we emphasize on doing far more than being, which is to our disadvantage.

Doing is about achievement, priorities, and goals—making stuff happen. Being is about self-awareness, caring, and creating a supportive culture of talent development. I once read an article about two successive governors of the same state and how their staffs regarded them. Governor A (let's call him) was hard driving, achievement oriented, and laser focused. His staff worked hard because they feared him. Governor B was self-aware, caring, and supportive. His staff worked hard because they didn't want to let him down. Which leader would you want to work for?

A leader must point teams in the right direction to get the job done and to be a mindful leader whom people want to follow. Many of us have gone on successful journeys with leaders and accomplished their visions. However, all too often after completing a task with a leader, people have often emphatically said: "Never again!" Such a leadership model is unsustainable. First, high turnover, the result of a never-again mind-set, costs anywhere from five to ten times the salary rate. Second, turnover is exhausting for both the leader and staff. High turnover indicates poor leadership. Indeed, people do not leave companies; they leave bad leaders—Gallup and others have data to support this.[34] Leaders must set a vision and a course and move people toward it. This requires both doing (making priorities happen) and being (being self-aware and other-aware—developing talent).

Leadership Roles—The Doing and Being Matrix: If you accept the notion that effective leaders must be both capable doers and decent, caring human beings, then the next diagram will make sense. Note that on *Y*-axis is "doing" from low (bottom left of the box) to high (top left). And on the *X*-axis is "being" with low (bottom left) and high (bottom right). The term for doing this is "effectiveness"—getting the job done. Also, the term for being is "likable," which might seem soft to some people. However, research strongly suggests that being implies self-awareness and other-awareness that leads directly to empathy and compassion. Ultimately, such self- and other-awareness produce a likable leader whom people will stick with, even when more money is offered by others.

- **Box #1 (Low Being and Low Doing): Unlikable and Ineffective**. These leaders probably should consider a different profession or role! Such poor leaders might require replacing, not just more training. This is especially true if such a person has been in place for some time and shows little appetite for positive, adaptive change.
- **Box #2 (High Being and Low Doing): Likable but Ineffective**. The leaders in this box are the "good buddy" types who want people to like them. If you ever watched the show *The Office*, Michael Scott is the consummate good buddy who never got much done. To help these leaders, offer them a 360-degree review and coaching. However, unless you can motivate these leaders to focus more on task completion and less on popularity, you may want to counsel them into another position that is a better fit.
- **Box #3 (High Being and High Doing): Likable and Effective**. These leaders are the superstars. People rarely leave their teams, and others want to be on their teams. A leader who

gets things done and develops people along the way is a great leader. You may want to clone this person!

- **Box #4 (Low Being and High Doing): Unlikable but Effective**. These leaders get the job done somehow, often by the force of their overbearing personality, but followers leave in droves. They elicit the never-again response mentioned previously. To help

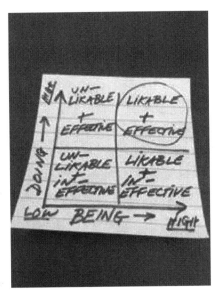

these leaders, conduct a 360-degree review, and they require further coaching. If they don't respond well to those efforts, counsel them into a new position that is a better fit—they often thrive as individual contributors.

As mentioned, if people are high at being and doing, keep them, reward them, and clone them! However, less effective and/or unlikable leaders may benefit from coaching.

Mindfulness and Coaching

As leaders, coaches, and humans, we get distracted—a lot. In fact, we have an evolutionary, survival need to access information, which often distracts us in the process of surviving! We forage for new and vital information, much like food foraging. And, such new information triggers our brain's reward—dopamine system. Unfortunately, modern-day access to huge volumes of information creates a brain overload and the frustration associated with it.

In *The Distracted Mind,* the authors outline how we get distracted, especially in this e-world full of competing images and sounds. The big problem: our ability to set goals is far more evolved than our goal-enactment abilities.[35] That's why it's much easier to set a weight-loss goal than it is to accomplish it. And given the amount of e-interference today, goal frustration looms over us constantly. So when working with coaching coachees in person, by phone or by video, coaches must contend with the distraction of their coachees and themselves as well.

Because the coaching process—discussed in the upcoming two chapters—is based on asking questions to cause reflection, it is inherently more mindful than most forms of communication. To ask a good question—one that causes the coachee to stop and reflect—the coach must also be in a mindful, present state. And again, Jon Kabat-Zinn defines such mindfulness as follows: "Being mindful means paying attention in a particular way: on purpose, in the present moment, and non-judgmentally." Further, when both the coach and coachee can be in that mindful place that Kabat-Zinn describes, great results are far more likely happen—more self-discovery and surprising "aha-moments," my personally most rewarding moments as a coach.

Jonathan Passmore, psychologist, researcher, and coach, has written on the positive effects of mindfulness on coaching and suggests four techniques to enhance the coaching experience by using mindfulness to prepare for coaching, to sustain focus in coaching, to keep attentive but detached during coaching, and to teach coaching to coachees.[36]

Prepare for Coaching

Like most people today, leader-coaches often find themselves in a mindless state—rushing from one appointment to another, commuting, and just living life with all its distractions. Getting into a mindful state of mind requires being intentional, even systematic. As a coach himself, Passmore understands the realities of balancing a career and coachees. He uses a four-minute mindfulness meditation prior to meeting with the coachee as a way of settling into a mindful coaching session. As a coach, I use a three-minute sitting mediation. As a leader-coach, you will need to settle down and become mindful before meeting with employees/coachees so that you and they are completely present and listening. There are any number of mindfulness apps, recordings, even YouTube videos (for of all sorts of time lengths) on the Internet. The key is to establish the intention and habit of mindfulness coaching. After my preparation mindfulness exercise, I then review my file notes from the previous session, especially the coachee's commitments to act. This simple process makes these commitments top of mind, of course, in concert with the coachee's most pressing need that day.

Stay Focused during the Session

Coaching sessions vary in length. Some coaches will use shorter thirty-minute coaching sessions, others as much as two hours. My general rule is to offer one-hour coaching if done by phone (about all my ear can take) and one hour and thirty minutes in person in my office. Without question, longer sessions require greater focus. Mindful focus on the employee/coachee makes for the best kind of coaching. However, with all the electronic devices in the environment, any leader-coach can get easily distracted. In my coaching practice, I clear my computer screen, turn off my cell phone, and put it away (just the appearance of it has been found by researchers as a huge distraction); and I breathe in a paced, mindful way—all the while, staying focused on one thing: the coachee's most important issue.

Be Emotionally Detached

Coachees are constantly going through major life changes that are often emotionally charged—fights within their teams or with colleagues. Such an emotional charge can be caught by coaches, if they're not intentional about remaining objective and emotionally detached. This doesn't mean being void of empathy, rather staying in a safe place that allows the coach to reflect and ask good questions to help the coachee work through this state to a more mindful one. Passmore says, "This requires the coach to both experience the emotions being felt by their coachee, but not to be flooded by them to the point where these emotions prevent the coach helping the coachee to move forward."[37] The job of the coach is to help the coachee become aware of the issues being faced and address them as necessary, not merely to be a supportive conversationalist. Thus, Hawkins and Smith (in Passmore) call this state "fearless compassion" that does not flinch from facing the issue at hand—despite the emotions associated with it.

Teach Coaching to Coachees

It is often said that we never really learn until we teach. This is never truer than with teaching mindfulness. For a leader-coach to help a coachee become more mindful, the leader-coach must develop a routine mindful practice as well as using mindfulness in day-to-day personal and coaching interactions. One way I teach my coachees is to give them a copy of one of my books titled, *Smile. Breathe. Listen. The Three Mindful Acts for Leaders* and ask them to read it—a short book that takes the average reader less than an hour. Then we discuss it at our next meeting—especially the section on breathing—focused on mindfulness. Then, I invite them to practice with me as a way of getting ready to settle in before coaching. Even just taking time to take three controlled deep breaths can help transition people from where they're coming from to the present—present in a safe place with their coach.

Note: The following chapters will explore coaching that is oriented toward both problem solving and talent development. It is assumed that leader-coaches described in the scenarios would be actively practicing and employing mindfulness, as described above. For the sake of conciseness, in the coaching scenarios presented in the forthcoming chapters, mindfulness tactics described above are not redescribed but very much assumed.

CHAPTER 3

How Is Mindful Leadership Coaching and Solving Problems?

M indful leader-coaches show up prepared to be completely present: undistracted, in the moment, listening with a nonjudgmental attitude, and focused solely on the coachee's problem or issue. However, as discussed above, leaders come in different flavors—there are infinite types and styles of leaders.

Types of Leaders

A host of leadership models are available, the result of numerous people trying to understand what makes good leaders. That said, one excellent explanation comes from Michael A. Germano, an attorney writing about leadership for the American Library Association.[38] I urge readers to read his article "Leadership Style and Organizational Impact." He does a remarkably succinct job of explaining some of the key leadership models. Below, I present a summary, as well as my own spin on his work. Let's consider the ABCDs of leadership.

- **Autocratic**. These leaders rule from a position of authority. "Do it because I say so" might be their mantra. This model works well in crisis and command situations like law enforcement, fire departments, and the military—when there is a good reason. However, if you use this dominant, restrictive model all the time, it quickly wears thin. People want and value autonomy.

- **Bureaucratic**: These leaders, often found in large organizations, operate from a prescriptive rule book—policies. In fact, their mantra might be "follow the policy." A bit like their autocratic brethren, they follow the rules, even at the expense of people. You find such people at local Departments of Motor Vehicles and other high-volume organizations. When such a bureaucratic, dominance model is used in for-profit organizations, it eventually results in the beginning of end-of-market dominance.

- **Charismatic**: These leaders have the personality and vision to motivate and inspire followers to work toward that vision. Their mantra might be "follow me toward the light!" They develop a creative atmosphere and loyal followers. By the force of their personalities, they eliminate any leadership competition. The result of their leadership style is that when they leave, a great leadership vacuum opens with no one to fill the void.

- **Democratic**: These leaders seek consensus on all matters. Their mantra: "if we're all affected by the decision, let's all vote on it." Unfortunately, this style can devolve into a vote-on-everything culture that is painfully slow and agonizing. Eventually, people get frustrated by the inaction and snail-like pace.

Now, there are myriad other leadership theories, such as transactional (goal and reward system), transformational (follower-based developmental process), situational leadership (morphing leadership to fit the maturity of the follower), emotional intelligence (self- and other-awareness), and so on.

However, over the years, I have observed several clusters of leadership approaches: command-and-controllers, fixers, and coaches.

Command-and-Controllers

Both the autocratic and bureaucratic leaders fall into this category. They basically tell people what to do based on sheer authority or dogmatic policy. Either "do it because I say so" or "do it because the rules say so." In the end, the message is that they want you to execute how, when, and where they say so. In the short term, this approach is fast and efficient; however, it's both less efficient and ineffective in the long run. People ultimately resent authority and want autonomy, especially as they mature at work. Overplaying this leadership style annoys and alienates employees, particularly the top performers, who will leave.

Fixers

This cluster often looks charismatic or democratic—in sum, benevolent. They like to help and add value, often more than is necessary. They like you to consult with them before tackling a problem, especially an important one, so they can add value and provide "help." When a fixer touches the project, he or she will stay with it until you or they finish it. They love to give advice and direction. While meaning well, fixers are direct descendants of command-and-controllers.

Without a doubt both command-and controllers and fixers are successful, up to a point. Sure, they get things done and offer a sense of quality control. They act like training wheels on a bike and never let you fall. However, other unintended consequences arise from these two approaches. When leaders are so deeply engaged in projects, the work eventually exhausts them and limits their scalability. After about twelve and fifteen employees, command-and-controllers and fixers start to burn out. There is too much to handle, especially if you have your fingers in all the pies. Overinvolved leaders erode their followers' initiative and engagement, yet both are critical to success in a competitive environment. Over time, followers of such leaders become lemmings, stand in line for answers, do what the leader suggests or demands, and leave work on the dot. They disengage and eventually turn into bureaucratic robots or leave for greener, less-controlling, pastures.

Coaches

A third and far more effective leadership approach is to coach people to get projects completed well. Who says so? Not just me but Google. Indeed, Google conducted a massive study (Project Oxygen) to determine the common characteristics of their best leaders. Here is what they found:

> Project Oxygen found that a good manager (1) is a good coach; (2) empowers and does not micromanage; (3) expresses interest and concern in subordinates' success and well-being; (4) is results-oriented; (5) listens and shares information; (6) helps with career development; (7) has a clear vision and strategy; (8) has key technical skills.[39]

Google's analytics are quite rigorous and may well suggest that in our more information-based and data-driven economy, the leaders who are less directive and more coaching-oriented are more apt to succeed. My own practice-based experience at using coach-based leadership supports Google's findings. I have one exercise that always proves this point in an "aha!" way. Here's how it goes:

1. At the beginning of the seminar, I ask participants to think of the best leaders they have ever known. Then I ask them to write down three words describing how that leader made them feel. The list of words typically looks like this:

BEST LEADER—made me feel...

—Valued
—Important
—Heard
—Challenged
—Confident
—Like I mattered
—Smart
—Safe
—Capable
—Trusted
—Competent

The list goes on, but suffice it to say, the description of how the best leaders make us feel is an overwhelmingly positive charge.

2. Next, I teach them the coaching model below. During the class they are asked to role-play being a coach and a coachee using the coach-approach model. About ten minutes before the class ends, I ask them to list three words that

describe how being coached made them feel. I create a list of those feelings on a flip chart.

3. Finally, I post the new list next to the original, best-leader list taken at the start of the workshop. Then I ask the class what they observe. Recall that the first list was made about three hours before the second and in a different context. Participants examine them analytically, but it does not take them long to say almost in unison—they are *very* similar. Both lists have identical positive charges.

4. Then I ask them what they think that means. "Hmm," they say, again almost in unison. Depending on how much time we have, I let them struggle toward the observation and synthesis. However, if time is an issue, I ask them what the first list signified. They start by saying something like this: "it is a collective wisdom list where we as a group described how great leaders made us feel." Then I ask about the second list. The response will be that it is a collective wisdom list of how coaching made them feel. Finally, I summarize by asking, "Then is it fair to say that using coaching produces the same feelings (emotional response) that the best leaders do?" And that is when they all react with a big "wow!"

Coaching Caveat

A major observation and caveat about coaching is that it's probably got a bad reputation! Even though I wrote a book about it, as an experienced executive coach, I can assure you that the only resemblance between "effective leadership" coaching and the traditional use of the term as in sports coaching is pure coincidence and often misleading.

In traditional sports coaching, you have an experienced, skilled leader who typically tells you what to do. Sure he or she works with the athlete, but a sports coach typically operates as an expert adviser—more like a consultant than a true leadership coach.

Quality leadership coaching revolves around asking good questions, not giving advice. Using the coach-approach[40] to leadership, leaders become wise sounding boards: guides on the side, not sages on the stage. At the core of the coach-approach are questions, a process, and lots of patience.

All that said, let's next explore the leadership problem-solving coaching model in depth.

Mindful Coaching: The Leadership Problem-Solving Coaching Model

I have been writing and teaching about the coach-approach model for years. In fact, I wrote *The Coach-Approach Leader* to help people understand the leadership coaching process in a simple, effective model.[41] And while I still like, use, and endorse that book, I have made some significant modifications to the original model—enough to require an update. The distinctions are that I have renamed the coaching quadrants to better reflect what occurs during the process. Terms like "issue," "impact," "ideal," and "intention" have been replaced with "problem," "present" (state), "possible" (future), and "plan"—for greater clarity and precision. Moreover, I've added additional questions to include "why." This will be explained later. Finally, I have come to realize that it could be improved on and adapted not only to help leaders coach people in solving problems but also to coach them toward career development as well.

All that said, here's the new and improved coaching model:

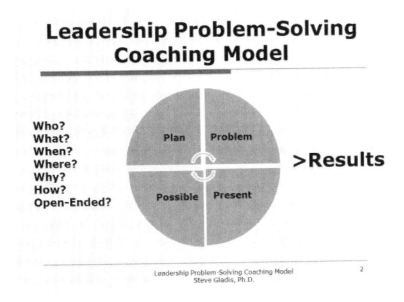

Leadership Problem-Solving Coaching Model

Who?
What?
When?
Where?
Why?
How?
Open-Ended?

Plan | Problem

Possible | Present

>Results

Leadership Problem-Solving Coaching Model
Steve Gladis, Ph.D.

2

Questions

Let's begin with questions, which is where all coaching ultimately begins. When I teach coaching, one of my favorite exercises is called "The TV Reporter." The exercise is used to teach leaders how to become "reporters" and ask great questions. In this exercise, each person pairs off with another in the class. They are given four to five minutes to interview their partner about what they did the day before. Then they must deliver an oral report in one minute entitled, "A Day in the Life of..." about the person they interviewed.

They each stand up; are given a five, four, three, two, one countdown; and are told to act as if they were on the nightly news. Everyone always enjoys this exercise! Many of them ham it up and try to outshine the previous reporter. Not only is this an engaging and entertaining exercise; it also demonstrates the best techniques of natural questioners and listeners: reporters.

If you have ever taken an introductory class in journalism or writing, the teacher probably taught the who, what, when, where, why, and how model, often called the 5Ws and an H. Such typical reporter questions focus on finding out "what's going on?"

I used to only allow my student "coaches" to ask who, what, how, and open-ended questions. I wanted them to focus on the questions that revealed the most information and were the least intrusive. I believed that leaving out when, where, and why not only simplified the process but also kept why out of the mix. In my experience as a federal investigator, I saw that why, if overused, makes an information-gathering session feel like an interrogation, not an interview. However, while I still teach students to underplay why, I tell them to use it when they feel it necessary and to use it more often as they gain experience and have a better understanding of the difference between interviews, interrogations, and cross-examinations!

Once you understand the notion of asking questions, you are ready to use the coach-approach process: a four-step model that guides anyone to have a thoughtful, mindful conversation with another. It's a mindful conversation for both the coach and coachee (person being coached); however, the process puts the coachee front and center. It's never about the coach teaching or consulting. Rather, it's about talking the coachee through a problem, issue, or concern to discover a path toward intention and action. The process is the result of research

42

and practice from my years of coaching, as well as the research and practice of other executive coaches.[42]

Let's examine the model, using a simple example to help illustrate the process.

The Problem

Everyone has problems! Some problems are bigger than others, but a problem causing an employee distress, distraction, or disruption needs to be addressed to help not only the employee but also the people in his or her life. Like throwing a rock in a pond, problems ripple and spread out from the individual, to associates, work teams, friends, and family. In fact, problems impact us twice as much as pleasures.[43] Most of us would gladly forgo a morning-kiss good-bye in exchange for not getting a speeding ticket on the way to work!

As a leader, it is important to help people solve their own problems without becoming engulfed or consumed by them. One technique to help you is to think about alligator arms! Picture alligators, which have very short forearms but longer legs. It would be very hard for alligators to "take on" someone else's problem because they would have trouble reaching out. Same should be true for the coach—don't take on coachees' problems. Rather, help them identify, solve, and be accountable for addressing their own problems. If you take on every problem that comes along and attempt to direct or fix it, you will quickly become exhausted.

A coach's job is to help the coachee identify the problem. This might sound odd because you probably think people know what is bothering them. But it *ain't necessarily so*! In fact, most people who come in for executive coaching know that they are upset, angry, and distracted—but they often do not know why. They clearly know the effects or symptoms of their distress but often don't know the real underlying problem. A good coach will probe the situation with questions to help the person reflect and discover the real problem, not just the symptom. In coaching, both the coach and coachee need to agree on the problem before proceeding. Until the coach can summarize the problem and get agreement from coachee, the questioning should continue. Coaching is an iterative process that ensures clarity and agreement on what the problem is before trying to solve the wrong problem! Here's a list of some questions coaches might ask to help discover the real problem or issue the coachee might have:

- Identify the issue or problem to discuss using the following questions:
    o What is the most important thing for us to discuss today?
    o What is an example of the problem?
    o Who, what, and how are others involved?
- Paraphrase the problem for agreement.
    o Is this the problem (*coach states understanding of problem here*)?
    o If not, discuss it further until agreement on the issue.

Note: A complete list of all the coaching questions can be found in the appendix of this book.

Let's use a hypothetical example to demonstrate the coach-approach process in action.

Situation: Marie is a thirty-five-year-old technical whiz with the highest level of government security clearances. This combination makes her extremely valuable to her current employer, XYZ Technologies, a federal government contractor. Indeed, her boss, Harry, wooed her for a year to entice her away from her former employer. Harry even had a celebration party with his team after he convinced Marie to sign an employment agreement.

However, a few weeks have gone by, and Harry has been on travel. When he returns, Harry walks by Marie's office only to observe her staring out the window. He approaches her and asks if she's OK. "Fine," she says in a monotone that indicates to Harry that she is anything but fine. Concerned, he invites her to lunch the next day.

Coaching Marie: The Problem: During a long and slow conversation, Marie admits to Harry that she's not feeling connected to her new job.

Fortunately, Harry has training as a leader-coach,[44] so he doesn't overreact but asks her a question: "So what's going on, Marie?"

She hesitates and says, "It's just not a great fit, Harry."

"Could you explain that a bit more, Marie?"

She explains that while she loves her work and the people are nice, she does not feel productive—not as able to get stuff done as she did in her previous job. Harry's questions uncover that Marie feels like the culture at XYZ is more extroverted than the culture at her previous company.

"It takes me almost twenty minutes to get from the parking garage to my office because people are so friendly and want to make me feel welcomed. Not that it's a bad thing, Harry, but, frankly, it's exhausting."

Harry listens intently and asks, "Anything else?"

She tells him that while her office mate, Pete, is a great guy, he is also quite loud on the phone. To drown him out, she constantly uses her earbuds at work and turns up her playlists as loud as possible.

Questions and answers continue as the story unfolds. The conversation continues for some time, and Marie reveals the following:

She is an achiever who loves to solve problems and get things done. She is also introverted and likes to work alone. She likes chatting with people, mostly one on one, after she has worked on the problem independently. She needs what she calls "think time" and dislikes small talk.

Listening intently, Harry says, "So to paraphrase what I think I heard you say, it sounds like the problem you're having is that you love to solve problems and get things done. You need time to do that independently, and you're not getting that here like you did at your former company. Is that it?"

She thinks for a second or two, smiles and says, "Yes. You nailed it, Harry."

Harry nods, smiles, and thinks, *Now we're getting somewhere.*

The Present State

Trained coach-leaders help coachees assess the present state of the problem by asking them questions. Often, coachees develop subtle problems over time. They not only don't know the real problem; they also don't recognize the impact the problem has on others around them. Often people underplay their problems, but a good coach, asking the right questions, can get to both the root problem and its magnitude and impact.

This is the time in the coaching session that the coach helps nail down the extent of the problem—who is being affected by it, how big is it, and so on. In addition, depending on the extent of the issues uncovered during coaching, there may be a need for multiple sessions, each building on the previous one. Here are some questions to determine the present state of a problem, to be used at each coaching session.

Present State:

- What impact is this issue having on you today?
- On others?
- On a scale from one to ten (one = low and ten = high), what impact does the problem have on you?
- What are the consequences of continuing the current path or doing nothing?

Coaching Marie—The Present State: After identifying Marie's initial problem, *not being able to be as productive as she had been at her former company due to a different culture/atmosphere at XYZ Technologies,* Harry probes the present state to assess the immediate impact it's having on Marie.

"So what's the impact all this is having on you today?" Harry asks after sipping on his iced tea.

"Good question; let me think," she says, looking up as if to search her brain. Then she explains that her work situation frustrates her, and she has brought it home to her husband and talked about it with her friends.

"So it's affected you and others around you?"

"Yes, I think I'm spreading negative feelings. And I hadn't noticed it until now."

"On a scale from one to ten—with one being low and ten being high—can you estimate how big a problem this is for you?"

"Hmm. I don't know, maybe a seven or eight. Actually, as I think about it, it's probably closer to a nine!"

Harry acknowledges the serious nature of the problem and then asks, "What are the consequences of just letting it ride? Doing nothing?"

"Frankly, Harry, I'm really thinking about calling up my former boss."

"I see. Sorry you feel that way," Harry calmly and with empathy says, as he thinks about his next line of questions and the possible future state.

The Possible Future State

Once the leader-coach has identified how serious the present state is, he or she will want to get the coachee focused on the best possible future state. Without a vision of the future, there's no target to aim at—and thus the goal is impossible to reach. The coach's job is to ask questions that allow the coachee to focus on what could be. We know from research on power and powerlessness[45] that when we feel like we can control our future (even by simply imagining it), we become energized and capable of making change. On the other hand, if we feel like victims and perceive that locus of control is external, we feel helpless and spiral down into a state of hopelessness. Here are some questions that will help the coachee focus on the best-possible future state:

- Understand the vision for success.
  o What would the best possible ideal state look like?
  o If a miracle happened and things were great, what would it look like?
  o What else?
- Set goals and performance expectations.
  o What do you want to accomplish?
  o What are some approaches you might envision?
  o What action might you take? What else?

- Identify possible resistance.
  - o   What or who are your major barriers?

Coaching Marie—The Possible Future State: After Harry helps Marie assess the extent of her problem, he prompts her to think about what would make things work better.

"Marie, what would an ideal work environment look like for you at XYZ Technologies?"

"Pardon?"

"Well if a miracle happened and tomorrow you came into work and things had changed for the better, what would be going on? What would have changed to make it great for you here?"

"I guess it would be quieter."

"What else?"

She thinks and says, "I'd have more control over my hours."

"And?"

"I'd have a quieter office mate or my own office?"

The conversation continues as Harry probes what Marie wants to accomplish and some approaches she could take. She tells him that she wants to contribute great analysis to the executives and government agencies that hire her for consulting work, do her job well, and get stuff done—one of her key strengths!

Harry then asks her to list some future actions she might take. After Harry suggests it, they brainstorm some ideas.

Marie says, "I guess could check out the nearby library. Maybe explore teleworking one or two days a week." She widens her eyes and adds, "Maybe even buy some noise-cancelling headphones!" Marie then shakes her head in mock horror, and she and Harry share a good laugh.

Further conversation yields a viable list of options. Finally, Marie smiles at Harry and says, "That was productive. Thanks, Harry!"

The Plan

A vision without a plan or intention going forward is like a car without a driver or, in my case, a car without a GPS! We all need to be specific if we are ever going to get things done. Classic goal-theory calls for SMART goals: specific, measurable, attainable, relevant, and time-bound. It is critical not to make this step onerous. As Beth Cabrera, one of my colleagues at George Mason University, often says, "Do less than you think you can do." The key is to start small—but mostly to start! Make the first steps easy and intended primarily to get the ball rolling. The key in this intentional planning step is for the coachee to commit to do something. The coach's job is to ask for that commitment by asking three questions: "What will you do? When will you do it? How will I know you did it?" These questions nail down accountability—the bedrock of effective coaching. Finally, I always ask a closing question at the end of each session:

"What is one thing of value that you got from this discussion?"

Here are the questions you can ask when you get to the planning stage of the coaching process:

Plan or Intention

- Agree on a plan, timeline, and accountability.
  o What will your first steps be?
- Enlist support from others.
  o Who can support you going forward?

- Set milestones and accountability.
  - o What will you do first? What do you want to be held accountable for?
  - o When will you do it?
  - o How will I know you've accomplished it?
- Assess impact of coaching.
  - o What's one thing of value that you got from this discussion?

Coaching Marie—The Plan: After asking Marie questions relative to the possible future state, Harry now guides her toward the next step—coming up with doable next steps.

"OK, Marie, you mentioned several possible steps you might take to get started on solving this issue. Which one would be the easiest one to tackle?"

"I could do a few easily."

"Yes, but let's start with just one step to get the ball rolling."

"OK. I'll check out the public library on Main Street to get the general feel of the place. I used to study in the library when I was in college. The dorms were a living hell to study in!"

"I agree. I'll support you on using the library anytime—of course, only for unclassified assignments. If you require any additional support along the way, just ask."

"Thanks, Harry. I appreciate your helping me think this through."

"Great. When do you think you might have a chance to check out the library?"

"I have some open time tomorrow afternoon."

"Great, can you let me know what you find after you scope it out? Maybe stop by the office or send an e-mail."

"Sure, not a problem. I'm actually excited about my field trip!" she said with the first genuine smile Harry had seen all day.

"Can I ask you just one final question?"

"Sure."

"What's one thing of value you got from our discussion today?"

"Good question," she said. "Well there was a lot. But the big thing I got today was hope."

"Hope?"

"Yes, hope for the future. That maybe I can figure this out? It's been a problem for me since grade school. It's time I mastered it."

"Great. Happy to help."

———

Now, simply going to the local library may not seem like a big step forward, but it is. Getting someone to commit to take the first step toward a goal may be the biggest step they'll take. So make it easy.

Coaching is iterative, and a coach takes small, but regular, bites of the apple. The more severe the issue, the quicker the testing of the "bites." So Harry will need to have multiple coaching sessions with Marie and, possibly, with Pete, her office mate. He also suspects that the library will be a temporary solution that will wear thin rather quickly. That will need to be addressed as well.

With coaching, the more that can be done by the coachee, the better. This allows the coachee to learn more, feel more buy-in, take more control of the environment, and so on. Now that Harry is involved, he will see how far and how fast he can safely go with engaging Marie in solving the issue (the central point of coaching). However, as her supervisor, he will be prepared to step in to help when she needs it. It's like watching your kids solving problems with other kids at school and not jumping in too soon—but closely monitoring to make sure no one gets hurt.

So in future sessions, with Marie's permission, Harry might offer Marie options—for example, does she want to talk things through with Pete or have Harry do it? One factor is that if Harry does the counseling of Pete, it sets up a whole different set of dynamics between Marie and Pete. While the simple solution is to just move Marie, the corporate culture might well then reject her because private offices aren't part of the company culture. And culture is like the sixth person on a basketball team—the crowd—and has a *lot* of power organizationally. In addition, nobody likes to see the new kid on the block, even a superstar, treated as too special. So Harry is not going to create another problem if it is at all avoidable.

Regardless, Harry won't lose Marie no matter what he must do. He wants to make sure she's at XYZ Technologies for a long time. The coaching will continue until he is confident that that will be the case.

In the next chapter, we'll look at how you can also use coaching to develop people's careers—critical to everyone, especially young and up-and-comers.

CHAPTER 4

How Is Mindful Leadership Coaching Used to Develop Talent?

Without question, talent development is one of the greatest challenges facing employers today. The facts: baby boomers (born between 1946 and 1964) are reaching retirement age (sixty-five) to the tune of ten thousand a day![46] This mass exodus of baby boomers creates a talent vacuum, not because boomers are extraordinarily talented but because they have unintentionally dominated the workplace for so long. As one example of the importance of talent today, one of the country's premier associations, the American Association for Training and Development (ASTD), has changed its name to the Association for Talent Development (ATD). This was a well-thought-out, intentional decision made while looking at the horizon of global business. In a recent study by McKinsey, the bottom-line conclusion was that in the next twenty years, talent acquisition will be the top priority for all organizations and will result in an all-out talent war.[47]

Talent development has become an increasingly popular subject of newspaper, magazine, and journal articles. Large companies like Deloitte and the federal government have shifted their approach to performance appraisal from ritualistic, episodic events toward meaningful and frequent feedback sessions aimed at talent retention. Indeed, when people walk away from an organization, the costs are hidden and very expensive. Estimates for recruitment and training of a new employee range from 30 to 50 percent of salary (for entry-level positions) to over 400 percent times the salary for executives.[48] A company with a 10 to 20 percent turnover rate, especially among key players, can quickly go from being an industry leader to an industry laggard.

According to an article[49] by Jennifer Robinson in the *Business Journal,* managers sit at the center as the major cause of turnover. Referring to Gallup-based stats, she notes that turnover breaks down this way (note percentages have been rounded off): 17 percent leave because of their direct manager and the environment, 32 percent leave because of a lack of career advancement, 20 percent because of a lack of role fit, 22 percent for better pay and benefits, 8 percent because of a lack of flexibility, and 2 percent for a lack of job security. Notice how high a percentage the manager influences—a whopping 77 percent (17 percent—directly about the manager, 32 percent—lack of advancement, 20 percent—poor role fit, 8 percent—lack of flexibility). And, the best go first, because they can. They have options! Turnover of high potentials can kill you, although turnover of low potentials might actually be a good thing.

Thus, leaders need to take responsibility for retaining quality people. One great way to do that is to communicate with employees frequently about how they are doing, find out what they want to do, and help them find meaning and purpose in their work. And developmental coaching provides an excellent way to signal to high potentials that you care about them and want them to stay around and contribute.

One caution on the difference between problem-solving coaching and leadership developmental coaching: don't try to do both types of coaching in the same meeting. Often, supervisors will conduct an annual performance review, or problem-solving session, and tack on a career-development discussion. Doing this is often an attempt to be efficient—a kind of two-for-one opportunity. Warning: resist this temptation. Multitasking does *not* work. We have considerable data to prove and demonstrate this.[50] Leaders should absolutely conduct performance reviews but do so separately from career-development reviews. Moreover, conduct development reviews in a relaxed, informal setting—over lunch or coffee—which sends a message that the development meeting is a personal, me-and-you meeting.

Leadership Development Coaching Model

It is critical to conduct regular leadership-development interviews of everyone in the company, especially those with high potential. As mentioned, a failure to do so sharply raises the risk of turnover. The good news: if you know how to conduct leadership problem-solving coaching, you are already half-way home to learning leadership development coaching. We will use the same process in a kind of reverse way—starting with the possible future state first. Why? Because people's hopes and dreams for a better life lie in their future. Here's the model. Looks familiar?

The only difference from the problem-solving model is where you start the process and the direction of progression. Also, there is an increasing body of research around coaching toward a personal ideal state (personal vision) and the intense power a personal vision has on people. A key proponent of this method is leadership professor at Case Western Reserve, Richard Boyatzis, who has been at the center of this emerging theory—Intentional Change Theory (ICT).[51]

We will start an investigation of the *leadership development coaching model* with the possible future state and move toward the present state and its impact, then to the problem, and finally to the plan (see figure above).

The Possible (Future) State

As previously mentioned, leadership development coaching starts with the possible future state because most people are interested in future development. In fact, as mentioned before, 32 percent of people leave their jobs for lack of advancement. Paying attention to career advancement is not just something trending on Twitter or a nice afterthought; rather, it's critical to corporate success, even survival. Taking the time to tell employees how much you appreciate them and asking them what they want to become in the future is both empowering and a goal-setting technique. When people believe that they have control over their own destiny, they become empowered. Research by some of the best psychologists has demonstrated that this sense of personal control over destiny, combined with sheer grit, separates fixed (pessimistic) people from those who are growth (optimistic) oriented.[52] When people visualize their future, they are on a path to becoming grittier, smarter, faster, and better.[53] Here are a few sample questions that leaders might ask when coaching employees to understand their vision for success in the future in the time horizon they choose as most meaningful and important to them.

Questions about the Possible Future State:

- Ideally, where would you like to be in your career in the future?
- In what capacity (work) do you think you would flourish?
- Who would you be working with?
- Where would you be working?
- What would the ideal job look like?
- *(Coach summarizes and confirms the best possible future state about the coachee's career.)*

Let's use a hypothetical example to demonstrate the coach-approach process in action when focused on employee development.

The Situation: Will Sutton is a twenty-eight-year-old employee for a high-tech firm, Real-Time 1-2-3, which specializes in software development for companies managing user feedback on their sites, to get an accurate sense of how people like and perceive their products. The intelligence from this software helps clients target their sales efforts, gives them real-time feedback on how the product is performing, while simultaneously giving feedback to Real-Time 1-2-3 code developers to help modify the current products and even develop new products to give their clients a competitive advantage. Will has been with Real-Time for several years as a client liaison representative who reports back to technical developers on how client companies use the key software, Real-Time Sensor. Will is terrific at his job, and the company wants to keep him.

Coaching Will—The Possible Future State: Here is a conversation between Will and Janice, his supervisor and director of development for Real-Time 1-2-3.

Janice: "Will, thanks for having lunch with me today—my treat by the way."

Will: "Thanks. I appreciate the time and the lunch."

Janice tells him how much she and the company appreciate the great work he has done this past year. She mentions several specific examples of Will's work.

Will responds with a kind of "aw-shucks" shrug as he beams with a smile.

Then Janice asks him, "What do you want to do next in the company, Will?"

"Umm. Interesting question," he says looking up, caught off guard a bit by the question.

Janice helps by saying, "Let me add a clarifying question. What does your future ideal job look like? I mean, if you could, what would you be doing, who would you be working with, that sort of thing. With our company—needless to say," as she winks and smiles at him.

Will laughs and says, "Ideally, I'd still be working with clients, but fewer and larger ones. I'd also continue to work with the software-solution developer folks as well."

"Sounds like you want to be a client liaison between key customers and the key developers."

"Yeah, maybe a step or two up from where I am now. But I do love the customers and the software team and want to stay connected to both."

Janice asks more questions targeted toward getting Will to tell her specifically what he would most like to do in the future. He tells her about his interest in becoming more technically savvy, learning about programming—not so much to be a programmer, just to become more knowledgeable on the topic.

After about ten to fifteen minutes of discussion, Janice says, "OK, so if I have this right, you want to do the same kind of work you do now—as a kind of 'translator' between our top customers and our best developers. Is that it?"

"Yes, I...think you have it."

"You sound hesitant. Did I miss something or misstate something?"

"No, but I also like our liaison team—my coworkers. I'd prefer to stay on my current team but get a promotion. I hope that's a possibility."

"Thanks for the vote of confidence! And, as I recall, you are the best softball pitcher on our league team—so that's an important consideration!"

Will takes a mock bow, and they both laugh.

The Present State

Coaching that starts with the best possible future state primes employees to consider what is possible. Following that, taking an inventory of the employee's current career state will provide a baseline for moving careers forward toward the future. A discussion about the present state of activities and tasks—likes and dislikes—is necessary and not always comfortable. Change is about giving up old things and learning new things, both of which can be painful, regardless of how attractive the future goal appears. Mostly, there must be a realization that moving forward has an impact—some things are left behind and new challenges emerge. For example, graduating from college is both exhilarating but scary, because while you celebrate reaching a monumental goal, you also must leave it behind for an uncertain future.

Questions to Investigate the Present (Current) State of the Employee:

- Will you describe your current job and what it entails?
- When you are at your very best at work, what are you doing?
- What are your three best strengths?
- What are your challenges?
- If you moved to a new job, what might it look like?
- What would be the most difficult thing to let go? What else would be hard to give up?

Coaching Will—The Present State: Just as their lunch entrees arrive, Janice asks, "I think I have a pretty good idea of your work, but can you describe a typical day in your current job? Warts and all?"

Will explains that he generally arrives at work around 8:00 a.m., checks his e-mail for any urgent issues, and touches base with the webmaster about any current complaints or compliments on the site regarding the software and his clients. Then he checks in with the key project engineer to determine if any specific system glitches might play into any problems. Will continues to detail the rest of his workday to paint an accurate picture for Janice.

"So, Will, when are you at your best at work?"

"When I'm acting like MacGyver."

"Who?"

"MacGyver—he's a secret agent on TV, who can solve any problem. He was the most resourceful person on the planet. He could fix anything and make it work—often using random items—like duct tape and a wire coat hanger!"

"Sounds like a guy I could use at my house. My husband, Jack, and I are hopeless at do-it-yourself home improvement projects."

Will smiles and continues, "I love to keep things running. Do whatever's necessary, and then go back later for the permanent fix."

"That's one of the reasons why I value you so much," Janice says and then asks, "What do you think are your three biggest strengths?"

"I'm resourceful and analytical, I suppose. I love to take broken things apart, find the problem, and put them back together again. I need to think about the third one."

"Sure. I just wanted to get your take on what you think you're good at. That said, what challenges do you have at work?"

"Sometimes I get impatient with the bureaucratic system. And I'm not big on excuses. If something doesn't work for a client, it doesn't matter whose fault it is; it just needs to get fixed."

"Those sound like good problems to me."

"Yeah. But those challenges sometimes get me in rather heated discussions with people whose work philosophy differs, shall we say."

Janice smiled and said, "I understand." Then she looks directly at Will and asks, "What if we talk about existing positions at Real-Time 1-2-3? Which of them might you look at doing in the future?"

Will strokes his chin and focuses on a spot over Janice's shoulder and then says, "I'm not really sure the exact position exists. For example, the senior-analyst position has a lot of supervisory responsibility. I'm not sure that interests me right now. I guess we'd have to consider some modifications to get to my ideal next position," he says with a smile.

They then have a productive discussion about crafting a new job tailored for Will that would be an individual contributor position, not a supervisor. They come up with a working title—strategic client liaison—and discuss what that position might look like. They conclude that it might consist of Will working with the company's key, strategic client-partners to make their experiences extraordinary.

"If you moved up to a new position, what positive aspects of your current job would you have to give up?"

"I never thought of that," Will muttered. "I assumed I'd do more of the same. Well, on others. I'd have to give up some clients I like to focus deeply."

"How does that sound now that you're saying it out loud?"

"Weird. And rather uncomfortable."

"Do you mean that you wouldn't have as many opportunities to act like MacGyver with certain clients who you like?"

"I never thought of it that way, but yes."

The Problem

This phase of developmental coaching focuses on helping the coachee discern the gap between where he or she is right now (the present) and where the possible future lies. That gap leads to a set of objectives for the coachee to develop and use to navigate toward the future. To sum up where we are now in the process: The coach helps the coachee formulate a personal vision (the possible future state), assess where he or she is now (the present state), and define the gaps to get from the present to the ideal state (the problem/gap state). It is important to note that this developmental conversation is the first of several conversations that might take place. However, simply outlining broad goals in this initial discussion is a sufficient, even motivating start. The key is for Will to know that Janice appreciates him and cares about his future with the company.

Questions to Investigate the Problem State of the Employee:
These questions investigate the problem state—bridging the gap—for the employee to start moving from the current state toward the ideal state.

- What does the gap look like between where you now are and where you want to be in the best possible future?
- What questions do you have to answer to get from here to there?
- What are a few steps that might help you get to your best possible future?
- What are some approaches you might take? What else?
- Would it help for us to brainstorm?
- Who can you enlist to help you move toward your best possible future?

Coaching Will—The Problem State: As Janice puts down her coffee cup, she poses this question: "As you look at the possible new position of strategic key client liaison, what questions come to your mind about getting from where you are now to achieving your future career goals?"

Will scratches his head. "I'm not sure. Maybe this is the first step, just discussing it."

They both agree on that point, but with probing from Janice, Will admits that he's intimidated by the responsibility of dealing with major clients. And he is a bit fearful of the administrative process involved in modifying his job or creating a new one.

Janice says, "How about leaving all the admin stuff to me? I want you to focus on getting yourself ready for the job transition."

Will smiles and says, "I can't thank you enough."

Janice replies, "My pleasure. Now let's talk about what next steps are needed to get your transition moving."

Will has some trouble getting started but finally comes up with a few thoughts:

—He will need to research comparable positions in the industry and talk to some people about their duties. He will start by contacting some of his friends in the industry.

—He might need communication training to deal with more sophisticated clients.

Janice jumps in and says, "Would it help you if we brainstormed?"

"Yes!"

Janice begins, "I wonder if you will first have to sell your position to the tech and sales guys?"

Will adds, "Yes, and how much time out of the office will I need to spend at client sites? And, what other skills will this new job require?"

They brainstorm for a while, which yields a list of ten actions that Will can take. Janice follows up with, "Is there anyone you can ask to help you move to the next step. Any friends or colleagues?"

Will comes up with three people he can rely on—his buddy Sam, who works for another tech company and knows the space well; Harry, a more experienced coworker at Real Time who is near retirement; and Janice herself.

She nods in acknowledgment of the compliment and then says, "Great. Let's look at the entire list and put them in order of importance."

The Plan

Once the coachee establishes the gap (and steps to close it), going from where he or she is to the best possible future state, it's time to get busy. Indeed, the time has come to act and take the first step in the journey. The coach has a couple of functions at this point in the process. The first is to transition the coachee to action—but not too much action—by taking the first step. The idea is to push the coachee to take action but not take on something too overwhelming. Second, the coach needs to have several big questions answered to set milestones and get accountability:

Questions to Investigate the Plan Going Forward of the Employee:
These questions help to set milestones and accountability.

- What will you do first?
- What do you want to be accountable for?
- When will you do it?
- How will I know you've accomplished it?
- What's one thing of value that you got from this discussion?

Coaching Will—The Plan: Janice wants to help Will start his journey, so she begins by setting the stage.

"OK, Will, we've got quite a list here," she says showing him her iPhone screen with all his ideas ranked in order of importance.

"Wow," says Will, impressed with the list. "Can you e-mail that list to me?"

"Sure. As you look the list over, where do you want to start?"

"I want to do it *all!*"

"OK, but the best advice when it comes to starting something new is to go slow at first and do *less* than you think you can. Start small, but be persistent."

"Yes, but I want to start this position as fast as possible."

"Understood, but you don't want to burn yourself out in the process, either," she says with a smile.

"Thanks. I appreciate that you're focusing on the long term. Sometimes I get overexcited."

Janice smiles and says, "I know you're pretty busy this time of year. So what is one thing you could realistically do in the next few weeks?"

"I could call my tech friends who might know of any similar positions in the market that could be worth exploring, and I'll do come research on similar positions."

"That sounds like a good start. When do you think you might be able to get that done?"

"Next month—by the fifteenth."

"Would you please text or e-mail me when you've done that?"

"Sure. I'll text you."

"Great."

Janice also sets a date about two months from now to have a check-in meeting with Will over coffee to keep the ball rolling. Then she asks, "So as you think of our conversation today, what's one thing of value you got from it?"

"I got a lot out of it. Mainly, I really appreciate you taking the time to discuss my future. It makes me feel valued, like I really matter to the team."

Janice smiles and nods.

Will adds, "Also, I really can see a path forward and that feels really good. Thanks again."

"My pleasure for sure."

———

This is what a leadership-developmental conversation sounds like. It's a structured but naturally flowing conversation focused on one thing—the career of the individual being coached. Focused time on someone's career tells him or her that you care and that sends a powerful message.

CHAPTER 5

HOW IS MINDFUL LEADERSHIP COACHING USED WITH GROUPS AND TEAMS

Question: Have you ever heard anyone say, "We need more meetings in our organization"?

Answer: Are you kidding?

Most people would eliminate as many meetings as possible. An article in a recent issue of *TD Magazine* reports that 75 percent of all midmanagement employees spend between three and four hours a day in meetings.[54] Meetings are a time and energy sinkhole! To cut down on the number of meetings, make them count and get something done. Fortunately, when you apply the coaching process to any meeting, it changes them dramatically. Whether it's a team meeting or a large group gathering of people trying to solve a problem, making people more mindful and reflective by asking questions in a systematic way changes the game.

Groups require coordination, and the larger the group, the more coordination required—you need a traffic cop of sorts to direct, but not drive, the traffic. Thus, the big difference from one-on-one coaching is that with a team or group, a coach facilitates the process, requiring questions and the coaching process to evolve.

The roots for good team or group coaching lie in a process called "action learning," originally developed in England by Reg Revans and refined over the years. Then a doctoral student at the world-renowned Cavendish Labs at Cambridge University in England—home to twenty-nine Nobel Prize winners—Revans captured their largely inquisitive discovery process, codified it, and developed a replicable process for companies. His work has been refined and developed in the United States by scholars such as Michael Marquardt at The George Washington University, who has taught the process widely and founded the World Institute for Action Learning to spread the word. With some simple rules and discipline, this process can be adapted quickly to most meetings.

The basic several-to-one requirements include the following:

- **Coach**: You need someone to act as the "coach" in charge of the process but not directly participating in the problem solving.
- **Participants**: Four to eight people works best. If you have fewer than four people, you lose the power of cognitive diversity—people thinking differently about the same problem. With more than eight people, you have trouble just getting the meeting to happen.
- **Rules**: Just few simple rules:
    o The coach can stop and start the meeting at any time.
    o Participants may only speak if responding to a direct question.
    o Anyone can ask anyone else in the group a question.
- **Questions:** Should be open and information-seeking. Questions like who, what, how, when, and even why and open-ended questions are best.

- **Process**: Using the coach-approach process works well: problem, present, possible, and plan.

What follows are two ways to use coaching both for team coaching (several-to-one coaching) and group coaching (one-to-many coaching).

Several-to-One Coaching

Just as one-on-one coaching provides an opportunity to reflect and thoughtfully solve problems, several-to-one coaching amplifies the experience. In essence, four to five people coaching one person happens best with one of the participants acting as the "managing coach" ensuring that the other coaches follow the coach-approach process—asking questions, not giving advice. Sounds easy, but when you increase the number of participants in the coaching process, the job of the managing coach becomes critical to success. It's like the difference between having one child or having three. One child is a big wave in the ocean of your life, but three is like a tsunami!

Following the general rules listed above (see "The Basic Several-to-One Requirements"), here's what a typical many-to-one coaching experience might sound like:

Situation: Richard has just been hired as the director of business development for a small and growing department of defense focused company in Washington, D C. This firm wants to expand into commercial technical contracting to widen and diversify its revenue base. Richard has direct and current experience working in a commercial technical consulting firm where he headed business development and did a great job. Thus, he offers his new company the kind of experience it's seeking.

However, this is Richard's first encounter with government contracting—a much different animal. The CEO nonetheless believes that Richard has the both the mind-set and drive to make a big difference.

To make his transition smooth and teach Richard about government contracting, the CEO has asked Jack, a senior director at the company, to facilitate a coaching discussion with Richard and four other key players in the company: Abe, a key sales guy; Bill, the pricing expert; Claire, the CFO; and Diane, the marketing director.

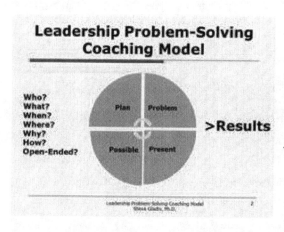

Jack opens the meeting by introducing everyone in the meeting and noting their corporate functions. Richard has met them all before, but Jack takes his time to make the group comfortable and at ease. Jack also reviews the "basic several-to-one requirements" (in the previous section), which all present but Richard are familiar with because the company started using this process a year ago, when the CEO returned from an executive coaching seminar at George Mason University. Finally, Jack points to the framed picture of the coaching model on the wall, as if to say, *Remember the process folks.*

Jack: "OK, let's get started. Richard, can you state the problem in a minute or two that you're facing as the new director of business development?"

Richard: "Sure, and thanks to everyone here today. I really appreciate your help. So basically, I'm trying to get my hands around government business development. I'm good with commercial development but must get my sea legs with government contracting—to learn how I can adapt it to the commercial world."

The Problem

Jack: "So who has the first question about the problem for Richard?"

Abe: "Well, I've been in on both sides, commercial and government, and I can tell you—"

Jack breaks in and says, "Abe, remember the rules. So what's the question you're answering or what question do you want to ask Richard about the problem?"

Abe: "Oops, sorry. My question is what do you already know about the government contracting process?"

Richard explains that he's taken several government contracting courses at the George Mason Enterprise Center through the Procurement Technical Assistance Program (PTAP), read quite a bit, and so on but has never sold directly to the federal government.

Diane jumps in. "It might help to know what's bothering you most. Can you share some of your questions with us?"

Richard asks several questions about their contracting process and major government regulations relating to those contracts, and finally about what he needs to learn to get up to speed fast.

After fifteen minutes of discussion, Jack reenters the meeting and asks Richard and the others to write down what they individually see as Richard's core problem or issue. Next, Jack asks everyone to respond, with Jack himself being last. Jack requires people to only read what they have written, which allows Richard to hear independent thought.

The comments vary from "Richard needs a fast-track course in government contracting" to "I hope Richard can get up to speed fast enough."

Richard listens intently and appreciates the questions. Finally, with more discussion, both Richard and Jack agree that, for the purposes of this meeting, Richard wants to know what he needs to know—critical information about government contracting—not just to survive but to thrive at his new job.

The Present

Jack then points at the coaching model on the wall again this time to the second step, the "Present" portion of the model. Then he says, "OK, who has the first question about the present state and its impact?"

Several questions come: "Who's affected by your success?" "What have you done before in similar situations?" "What's the most important thing for you to get a handle on first?" "On a scale from one to ten (one is low, and ten is high), can you put a value on this problem and its impact on you and others?" Finally, Claire, the accountant, asks, "What the single most important thing for you to master in the first month?"

Richard answers the questions and notes that the biggest thing for him to master in the next month is to clearly understand the bid proposal process. He also says that this ranks as a nine out of ten important problems for him.

Jack then asks Richard and the group, "So should the group discuss that as the key problem Richard is facing?"

Everyone, including Richard, nod their heads affirmatively.

Jack says, "Richard, can you restate this as a problem?

Richard responds, "Sure. In the next forty-five days, I need to clearly understand and be able to apply the bid-proposal process to be successful as the VP of Business Development."

The Possible

So moving forward, Jack points to the "Possible" part of the circle and asks, "Who would like to ask the first question about the best possible future state?

Diane, the marketing director, speaks up: "Richard, in forty-five days, if things went well, what would have happened?"

Richard: "Hmm…I guess I would have taken a couple of crash PTAP courses and talked to several successful BD folks from other noncompeting companies. Also, I'll want to start talking to current clients and seek their advice and of course talk to the CEO, my staff, and all of you! And by the way, what else have I forgotten to say?"

After being invited to speak by Richard, each of the participants volunteers to help and gives him suggestions about online courses, free counseling from the SBA, and several other solid recommendations.

When Jack sees the momentum stall, he points back up at the model to the "Plan" section and asks, "How about any questions about next steps?"

The Plan

Abe asks if Richard sees any obstacles that lie ahead.

Richard: "Just my ability to drink from a firehose of information!"

Everyone laughs.

Bill, the pricing guy, asks, "Besides us and the CEO, is there anyone else who might help you get jumpstarted?"

Richard replies, "I think the George Mason PTAP folks will continue to be a great help."

A few more questions come, and then Jack asks, "OK, how about specific questions about accountability?"

That's when Claire pipes up as if reciting from a script: "OK, so let me be the one to ask you the three *big* accountability questions. In the next couple of weeks before we get back together:

1. What will you do?
2. When will you do it?
3. How will we know you did it?"

Richard pauses to reflect and then says, "OK. I will get to Mason and enroll in another course. I'll go online and search for other educational options. I'll come by and talk to each of you. And... well I think that's plenty, given that I'm also going to be doing a lot of client meetings. I'll have all that done and can report back to you all in two weeks when we meet again."

Jack takes some notes and says, "Great. Let's all meet in two weeks—same time, same place. I'll send out a calendar request. And thank you, Richard, and all of you for participating today."

Following this meeting, the group will likely meet a few times to make sure that Richard is up and running well. Jack might just conduct one-on-one coaching from then on. It all varies depending on the progress toward the goal of Richard thriving as the new head of business development.

One-to-Many Coaching

If you've ever sat through an endless, painful, and rambling committee or staff meeting, the one-to-many coaching technique will make you want to jump with joy. The critical problem with most group meetings, regardless of size, is a woeful lack of both a structure and an approach focused on mindful reflection. As in several-to-one coaching, one person must fill the role of "managing coach" to ensure the group focuses on the coach-approach process—asking questions, not giving advice. And with a much larger crowd in the room, the managing coach acts like a traffic cop at the center of a busy intersection—keeping cars flowing, stopping some, and waving on others—per a proven process.

The Situation

The City Chamber of Commerce boasts of having over one thousand members and represents most of the largest companies in the region. The chamber has become a powerful business organization in the region; however, many small businesses believe that the chamber has abandoned its business needs in favor of catering to larger businesses. So the chamber CEO has hired an executive coach, Kimberly Gladwell, to help them work through this

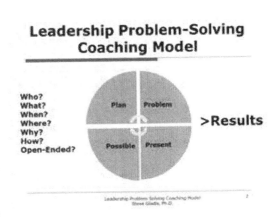

Leadership Problem-Solving Coaching Model

Who?
What?
When?
Where?
Why?
How?
Open-Ended?

Plan   Problem

Possible   Present

>Results

Leadership Problem-Solving Coaching Model
Steve Gladis, Ph.D.

problem. Kimberly is an experienced coach and an excellent facilitator.

With over thirty small business CEOs and senior executives in a large conference room, Kimberly calls the meeting to order. She takes ten minutes to introduce the purpose of the meeting and to explain the Leadership Problem-Solving Coaching Model posted prominently on the front wall of this large meeting room. Then she walks them through the process.

Kimberly: "To engage all of you to help address the chamber's services to smaller companies, I'm going to divide you into six groups of five."

With that she asks them to count from one to six and then repeat that process until every attendee has a number. Then she has all the ones get in a group, all the twos in another group, and so on. She does this to ensure that people don't end up talking to someone they came with and will get a chance to meet other people.

The Problem

Next, Kimberly points to the first step in the coaching process (the Problem) and asks the group, "Please discuss what you all think the problem is that we should be working on today. What does your group believe the biggest issue to resolve might be? Please start by each of you first writing down what *you* think the problem is and then just go around each of your groups reading what you've written before you begin to discuss it in your groups—so everyone's independent thoughts get heard first. So now please write out the key problem(s)—as you see them—on a piece of paper or on your smartphones. Take ten minutes to discuss everyone's ideas in your group, and then I'll ask each group to report out what they agree is the one biggest issue or problem."

For a bit, the room goes quiet as they write out their thoughts. After a minute or two, discussion erupts almost simultaneously from all six groups. Kimberly smiles as she walks and listens to each group.

When time is up, each group's designated spokesperson calls out their issues.

A. The chamber needs to stop catering to big companies.

B. The chamber needs to offer small businesses more reasons to become members and stay members.

C. The chamber owes us (small businesses) a lot. We are the backbone of the economy and the key source of creating new jobs.

D. The chamber needs to provide more small business programs.

E. The chamber should help us grow our businesses.

F. The chamber should forget big business and get back to its roots—small business.

Kimberly then asks the six groups to rank order and prioritize these six issues from one to six—where number one is the top issue they see and number six is the bottom issue. The group discusses and votes in the next five minutes and reports back to Kimberly, who tallies the results.

The clear winner by a big margin is issue B: *The chamber needs to offer small businesses more reasons to become and stay members.*

The Present

Kimberly points to the second quadrant of the coaching model and asks each of the six groups to take a moment and silently read a printout of services specific to small business prepared and distributed to all present by the chamber staff.

Kimberly: "I want you to do several things first on your own:

1. Please read over these offerings.
2. Then write down what programs or services for small business are missing from the list.
3. Consider the impact your suggestions might have on small businesses.
4. On a scale from one to ten (one is low and ten is high), please note your level of satisfaction with the current state of small business programs at the chamber."

Once the groups have done that, she asks that they come to some sort of consensus as a group on maybe three to five suggestions to augment the chamber list. She gives them fifteen minutes for this exercise. Each group is given some sticky flip-chart paper and markers to consolidate their team's response.

Finally, she says, "Also, pick a new spokesperson, rather than the first person who reported out when you identified the problem."

Again, the groups go silent—this time for about five minutes—and then come to life quickly with energetic and engaged discussion.

Following energetic discussion, subsequent facilitation, and winnowing by Kimberly, she lists the following choices that emerged:

A. The chamber already offers more than we thought.
B. The chamber needs to have more sessions like this one for interaction and input.
C. We need to form an ongoing small business advisory group to keep small business needs at the forefront of the chamber.

The Possible

Next, Kimberly points to the third quadrant of the coaching model—The Possible.

Kimberly: "Now, I'd like you individually to kind of brainstorm any possibilities you see the chamber possibly offering in the future to help small businesses. Write down whatever comes into your head. Don't set any boundaries. Let's take about five minutes to do that, and then I'll tell you what to do with those ideas."

There is intense focus from the groups and a lot of smiling as they write down all the possibilities.

Next, Kimberly instructs the groups to have each member offer his or her best ideas one at a time. They are to offer just one idea and then move to the next person so that everyone gets a chance to talk. They can go around as many times as they like. When finished, they should write out their top five ideas, with the most important first. The groups get ten minutes and have to report out to the entire group.

All this happens, and the six groups produce a list of ten new ideas—many of the suggestions were redundant or didn't stand the pressure of the vote as each member in the large group forced-ranked them from one to ten (one low and ten high).

Some of the ideas were as follows:

1. Start a small business advisory group at the chamber.
2. Develop a small business executive forum with great speakers to help small business executives stay on top of critical business issues.
3. Come up with a leadership development program for small businesses to help prepare leaders for the future.

There are lots of engagement and smiles during this exercise!

The Plan

Kimberly describes the next step as "where the rubber meets the road." She explains that it's fun and important to come up with new ideas. However, the ideas need to be executed, or they just wither on the vine. This next step focuses on what the next steps should be.

She gives the three ideas identified in the Possible step to the six groups, having two groups that will work on each problem independently. She notes the obvious redundancy but explains that the groups will be combined after the next round. It's important to keep as many people as possible engaged at this stage of the process.

Kimberly then asks the groups to go back in session and answer three key questions.

1. What actions will they commit to doing regarding their issue?
2. Will they be able to get them done in a month?
3. Will they be willing to present to the entire group then?

The groups get right to work. In fifteen minutes, they have lists of things they'll do, they agree on a date for a second meeting, and they agree on a leader to present the findings.

Finally, Kimberly asks everyone to write down one thing of value they got from the workshop today. The room goes quiet as they write or text on their phones.

Kimberly: "Anyone willing to share what they wrote?"

About fifteen hands enthusiastically push up into the air. Kimberly smiles, as she listens to what they have to say.

CONCLUSION

Coaching has evolved into a legitimate, modern coaching model. And mindfulness has likewise emerged as a powerful leadership lever. Combining these two elements makes each more powerful—like combining hydrogen and oxygen to create the life-giving force, water.

This book is a conscious attempt to introduce mindfulness (being fully present) to leaders in a simple and direct way and then demonstrate how coaching might be the best leadership use of such mindfulness.

I'm going to stick my neck out here and predict that the mindful coach-approach will become the default leadership model of this century. Why? Because the more complex, technical, and global issues we tackle will require less of a yes-no, black-and-white, right-wrong sledgehammer approach. Complex issues require thoughtfulness, not haste and reflection, not a knee-jerk reaction. Coaching forces thoughtfulness and reflection like no other technique.

However, we were all born with an amygdala, which doesn't simply react to surprise and change; it *over*reacts to surprise and change. As the threat detector in our brain, it predisposes us to reaction, not reflection, and thoughtlessness, not mindfulness. Being aware of our natural bias to reaction is important. Use of a simple but powerful technique—one that slows us down and causes us to reflect—gives mindful coach-approach leaders a powerful competitive and human edge.

While teaching this approach recently at a large US corporation, I said that if I could only teach one subject for the rest of my life, I would choose to teach coaching because it has such a huge impact on people, teams, and organizations.

I'm sticking with the statement.

What follows are two simple coaching forms to be used in coaching. Print them out to use as a guide when coaching people.

The 4-Ps Leadership Problem-Solving Coaching Interview Guide

1. **The Problem**
   a. What is the most important thing for us to discuss today?
   b. What is an example of the problem?
   c. Who, what, and how are others involved?
   d. *(Paraphrase the problem for agreement.) Is this the problem (coach states understanding of problem here)?*

2. **The Present (Current State)**
   a. What impact is this issue having on you today?
   b. On others?
   c. On a scale from one to ten (one = low and 10 = high), what impact does the problem have on you?
   d. What are the consequences of continuing the current path or doing nothing?

3. **The Possible (Future State)**
   a. What would the ideal state look like?
   b. If a miracle happened and things were great, what would it look like?
   c. What else?
   d. What do you want to accomplish?
      i. What are some approaches you might envision?
      ii. What action you might take? What else?

4. **The Plan (Next Step)**
   a. Who can support you going forward?
   b. What will you do first? What do you want to be held accountable for?
   c. When will you do it?
   d. How will I know you've accomplished it?
   e. What's one thing of value that you got from this discussion?

The 4-Ps Leadership Developmental-Coaching Interview Guide

1. **The Possible (Future State)**
   a. Ideally, where would you like to be in your career in the future?
   b. In what capacity (work) do you think you would flourish?
   c. Who would you be working with?
   d. Where would you be working?
   e. What would the ideal job look like?
   f. *(Coach summarizes and confirms the best possible future state about the coachee's career.)*

2. **The Present (Current State)**
   a. Will you describe your current job and what it entails?
   b. When you are at your very best at work, what are you doing?
   c. What are your three best strengths?
   d. What are your challenges?
   e. If you moved to a new job, what might it look like?
   f. What would be the most difficult thing to let go? What else would be hard to give up?

3. **The Problem (The Gap)**
   a. What does the gap look like between where you now are and where you want to be in the best possible future?
   b. What questions do you have to answer to get from here to there?
   c. What are a few steps that might help you get to your best possible future?
   d. What are some approaches you might take? What else?

    e. Would it help for us to brainstorm?

    f. Who can you enlist to help you move toward your best possible future?

4. **The Plan (The Next Step)**

    a. What will you do first?

    b. What do you want to be accountable for?

    c. When will you do it?

    d. How will I know you've accomplished it?

    e. *What's one thing of value that you got from this discussion?*

Other Books by Steve Gladis

Positive Leadership: The Game Changer at Work

This book provides key research-based principles that will help you be a more effective leader. The first part of the book, "The Concept," gathers some of the best positive psychology research available and reads like a *Harvard Business Review* article. The second part, "The Story," is a leadership fable about a homeless former business executive who attempts to climb back into society after a shocking body blow to his life. The research and the story together make a memorable read.

Solving the Innovation Mystery: A Workplace Whodunit

In a virtual and fast-moving world, companies and people must become more adaptive and competitive or risk becoming obsolete and going out of business. The question is: How do we discover and grow new innovations systematically and reliably while still producing the products and services that make money to keep the lights on and pay employees? In short: How does a company remain both productive and adaptive? *Solving the Innovation Mystery: A Workplace Whodunit* helps you solve the mystery of the innovation equation. He gets at the slower-moving truth of how innovation actually happens and shows why we must resist the hero's tale and the mirage of the "eureka" moment.

Smile. Breathe. Listen. The 3 Mindful Acts for Leaders

This book is for leaders at any level of the organization, who care about being the best leaders they can be. Written to be read in a one-hour, single sitting, this fast-read book focuses on the science around three mindful acts—smiling, breathing, and listening— which make leaders more fully present, aware, and thoughtful. Based on the science associated with these simple but powerful acts, this book explains how to execute each act. In fact, there are specific ways for leaders to smile, to breathe, and to listen. Written in clear and plain language, the research is also supplemented with a case study that demonstrates the impact of these three mindful acts. This book is a fast-read for both new and experienced leaders who want to add a powerful tool to their leadership toolbox.

The Coach-Approach Leader

This book is a leadership fable about an elderly businessman, Leon Bausch, who takes over a company and teaches the company about the coaching process as the ultimate leadership model. With the help of Leon's longtime friend, confidant, and executive coach, J. C. Williams, Leon teaches his executives how to help people solve their problems by asking them key questions. This inspiring leadership story allows the reader to absorb the solid content of the coaching process by attaching it to the backbone of heartfelt story.

The Trusted Leader

The Trusted Leader is a business fable about a new young leader, Carlos Lopez, who gets promoted to supervising his peers. He gets conflicting advice from his boss about how to take charge, and it backfires. Confused, Carlos seeks out the best leader he's ever known, Coach Jack Dempsey. The two agree to meet regularly at a local restaurant to talk about leadership. The coach teaches Carlos about how to lead, while Carlos and the coach learn about each other's secret, sad, but ultimately formative pasts. Finally, the coach teaches Carlos about the trust triangle—the critical key to leadership.

The Manager's Pocket Guide to Public Presentations

This book is an indispensable reference for managers and executives who find themselves in the unfamiliar and often-frightening position of having to give a public presentation. It is a compendium of tips that will help any manager learn the survival tactics of public speaking. A simple, quick read, based on the accepted theory and practice of rhetoric, it is also a confidence builder that will help any manager begin to overcome anxiety over public speaking.

The Manager's Pocket Guide to Effective Writing

Written communication is prevalent at most levels of business, but especially at the managerial level. Your writing may be grammatically and logically sound, but is it effective? Is it conveying your message with the concision and accuracy that makes you an effective communicator? Whether you're a manager in charge of a group of writers or just a person interested in improving your writing skills, *The Manager's Pocket Guide to Effective Writing* uses easy, practical how-to steps to help you write better and ultimately make a better impression on others.

WriteType: Personality Types and Writing Styles

Based on individual personality styles, this book's content provides new strategies for the four basic types of writers: the correspondent, the technical writer, the creative writer, and the analytical writer. Each person fits one of these well defined writing "types." Once readers learn their writing personality and follow the writing process suggested in the book, they find writing easier and less anxiety producing.

Contact Information

E-mail:	sgladis@stevegladis.com
Telephone:	703.424.3780
Location:	The George Mason Enterprise Center
	4031 University Dr., Suite 100, Fairfax, VA 22030
Website:	www.stevegladisleadershippartners.com
Leadership Blog:	Survival Leadershiphttp://survivalleadership.blogspot.com
Twitter:	@SteveGladis
YouTube	https://www.youtube.com/user/sgladis

ABOUT THE AUTHOR

Steve Gladis, PhD

A leadership speaker, author, and executive coach, Steve Gladis is an authority on the subject of leadership. CEO of Steve Gladis Leadership Partners—a leadership development company—he is the author of twenty-two books on leadership and a professor at George Mason University. His company works with businesses, associations, and US government agencies, and he speaks regularly at conferences and corporate gatherings. A former faculty member at the University of Virginia, Dr. Gladis also served as an FBI special agent and was a decorated officer in the US Marine Corps. His company donates a significant portion of corporate profits back to the community. His previous book, *Positive Leadership: The Game Changer at Work,* is available on Amazon.

NOTES

1. Jon Kabat-Zinn, *Wherever You Go, There You Are* (Hyperion, 1994).

2. David Rock, *Your Brain at Work* (HarperBusiness, 2009).

3. Daniel J.Siegel, *Mindsight* (Bantam, 2010).

4. Mark Williams, "Mindfulness," YouTube, April 3, 2012, https:// www.youtube.com/watch?v=wAy_3Ssyqqg.

5. Sonja Lyubomirsky, *The How of Happiness* (Penguin, 2008).

6. Daniel ToddGilbert, *Stumbling on Happiness* (Vintage, 2006).

7. Richard E. Boyatzis and Annie McKee, *Resonant Leadership* (Harvard Business Press, 2005).

8. ScottEblin, *Overworked and Overwhelmed* (John Wiley & Sons, 2014).

9. Ibid.

10. Kabat-Zinn, *Wherever You Go, There You Are.*

11. Adam Gazzaley and Larry D. Rosen, *The Distracted Mind* (MIT Press, 2016).

12. Ibid.

13. EckhartTolle, *The Power of Now* (Namaste Publishing, 1999).

14. Viktor E. Frankl, *Man's Search for Meaning* (Random House, 2011).

15. David Gelles, *Mindful Work* (Houghton Mifflin Harcourt, 2015).

16. Robert B. Cialdini, *Influence* (Prentice Hall, 2009).

17. Ibid.

18. *Daniel* Goleman, *"Social Intelligence,"* Talks at Google, 2007, https://www.youtubc.com/watch?v=-hoo_dIOP8k.

19. 19Boyatzis and McKee, *Resonant Leadership.*

20. Ibid.

21. DanielGoleman et al. *Primal Leadership* (Harvard Business Press, 2013).

22. Ibid.

23. MarcusBuckingham, *Go Put Your Strengths to Work* (Free Press, 2007).

24. DanielKahneman, *Thinking, Fast and Slow* (Macmillan, 2011).

25. Barbara Fredrickson, *Positivity* (Harmony, 2009).

26. *Wikipedia,* s.v. "Breakup of the Bell System," https://en.wikipedia.org/wiki/Breakup_of_the_Bell_System.

27. Kelly McGonigal, *The Upside of Stress* (Penguin, 2016).

28. Steve Gladis, *The Coach Approach Leader* (HRD Press, 2012).

29. Dan Gilbert, "Dan Gilbert: The Surprising Science of Happiness," TED Talk, February 2004, https://www.ted.com/talks/dan_gilbert_asks_why_are_we_happy?language=en.

30. Russell Hanson and R. Mendius, *Buddha's Brain* (New Harbinger Publications Incorporated, 2009).

31. M. Ricard, "Matthieu Ricard: The Habits of Happiness," TED Talk, February 2004, https://www.ted.com/talks/matthieu_ricard_on_the_habits_of_happiness?language=en.

32. Oxford and Maurice Waite, ed., *Paperback Oxford English Dictionary* (Oxford University Press, 2012).

33. Kabat-Zinn, *Wherever You Go, There You Are.*

34. JenniferRobinson, "Turning Around Employee Turnover," *Business Journal,* 2008, http://www.gallup.com/businessjournal/106912/turning-around-your-turnover-problem.aspx.

35. Gazzaley and Rosen, *The Distracted Mind.*

36. J. Passmore, "Coaching in Safety Critical Environments," *The Coaching Psychologist* 9, no. 1 (2013): 27–30.

37. Ibid.

38. *Michael* Germano, "Leadership Style and Organizational Impact,"*Library Worklife,* 2010, http://ala-apa.org/newsletter/2010/06/08/spotlight/.

39. Charles Duhigg, *Smarter Faster Better* (Random House Trade, 2017).

40. Gladis, *The Coach Approach Leader.*

41. Ibid.

42. *Laura* Whitworth et al., *Co-active Coaching* (Davies-Black Publishing, 1998).

43. Lyubomirsky, *The How of Happiness.*

44. Leaders who have received coaching training and understand the power of questions.

45. A. Cuddy, "Your Body Language Shapes Who You Are," TED Talk., June 2012, accessed August 31, 2017, https://www.ted.com/talks/amy_cuddy_your_body_language_shapes_who_you_are.

46. *Russell Heimlich,* "Baby Boomers Retire," Paw Research Center, December 2010, http://www.pewresearch.org/daily-number/baby-boomers-retire/.

47. C. Fishman, "The War for Talent," *Fast Company,* July 1998, http://www.fastcompany.com/34512/war-talent.

48. K. Borysenko, "What Was Management Thinking? The High Cost of Employee Turnover," TLNT, April 2015, http://www.ere-media.com/tlnt/what-was-leadership-thinking-the-shockingly-high-cost-of-employee-turnover/.

49. J. Robinson, "Turning around Employee Turnover," *Business Journal*, May 2008,http://www.gallup.com/businessjournal/106912/turning-around-your-turnover-problem.aspx.

50. Gazzaley and Rosen, *The Distracted Mind.*

51. Angela M. Passarelli, "Vision-Based Coaching: Optimizing Resources for Leader Development," *Frontiers in Psychology*, http://journal.frontiersin.org/article/10.3389/fpsyg.2015.00412/full.

52. Angela Duckworth, *Grit* (Vermilion, 2016).

53. Duhigg, *Smarter Faster Better.*

54. ATD Staff, "Not Another Meeting,"*TD Magazine*, December 2016.

Made in the USA
San Bernardino, CA
19 October 2018